# ASTORIANS

## ECCENTRIC AND EXTRAORDINARY

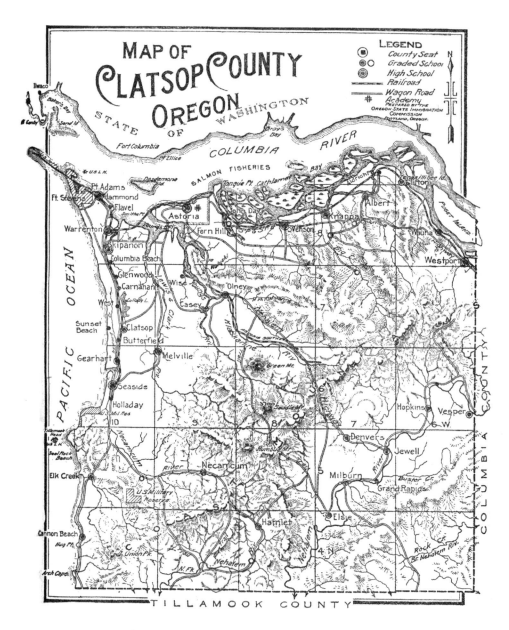

Map of Clatsop County prepared by the Oregon State Immigration

Commission of Portland, Oregon, 1915. CCHS COLLECTION.

# ASTORIANS
## ECCENTRIC AND EXTRAORDINARY

"FIRST FAMILY OF ASTORIA"

BY CALVIN TRILLIN

OTHER NOTABLE ASTORIANS BY

M. J. CODY

AMY HOFFMAN COUTURE

JOHN GOODENBERGER

NANCY HOFFMAN

LIISA PENNER

**EDITED BY KAREN KIRTLEY**

East Oregonian Publishing Company

Salem, Oregon

We are grateful to Sam Rascoe for organizing a
high-resolution image catalog. Tom Booth of OSU Press made many
excellent suggestions. Thanks are due also to John Bruijn, McAndrew Burns,
Alex Pajunas, and John Perry for their help in bringing this book together.

"First Family of Astoria" © 1993 and 2010 by Calvin Trillin.
"Other Notable Astorians" © 2010 by East Oregonian Publishing Company.
Images © 2010 individuals and collections as credited with each photo.
Compilation © East Oregonian Publishing Company in cooperation with the
    Clatsop County Historical Society.
Front Cover: *Harry at Home*, oil on canvas, 46" by 38", © 1991 and 2010 by R. Doane Hoag.
Back Cover: *Pier Astoria*, oil on canvas, 36" by 24", © 1990 and 2010 by R. Doane Hoag.
*Self-Portrait in the Schooner*, oil on canvas, 40" by 30", © 1993 and 2010 by R. Doane Hoag.

Distributed by Oregon State University Press, 121 The Valley Library, Corvallis, OR 97331,
541-737-3166
Toll-free orders: 1-800-426-3797


Library of Congress Cataloging-in-Publication Data

Astorians, eccentric and extraordinary / edited by Karen Kirtley.
    p. cm.
  Includes index.
  ISBN 978-0-87071-632-4 (pbk.)
    1. Eccentrics and eccentricities--Oregon--Astoria--Biography. 2. Astoria
(Or.)--Biography. 3. Astoria (Or.)--History. I. Kirtley, Karen.
  CT9990.A86 2010
  979.5'460922--dc22
                          2010028142


Editor: Karen Kirtley
Designer: Elizabeth M. Watson
Production Coordinator: Dick Owsiany
Photo research by Liisa Penner
Directed by Stephen Aldrich Forrester of the East Oregonian Publishing Company

Printed in the United States

# Contents

Introduction BY STEPHEN ALDRICH FORRESTER  7

PART 1

## The Magnificent Flavels  11

*First Family of Astoria by Calvin Trillin*

11

PART 2

## Other Notable Astorians  45

45

Coboway BY M. J. CODY  45

Donald McTavish BY AMY HOFFMAN COUTURE  52

Jane Barnes BY AMY HOFFMAN COUTURE  55

Robert Shortess BY AMY HOFFMAN COUTURE  59

John McClure BY AMY HOFFMAN COUTURE  63

Alexander Lattie BY AMY HOFFMAN COUTURE  66

John Shively BY NANCY HOFFMAN  69

69

Solomon and Celiast Smith BY AMY HOFFMAN COUTURE  72

Truman Powers BY AMY HOFFMAN COUTURE  75

William H. Gray BY AMY HOFFMAN COUTURE  77

Cyrus Olney BY NANCY HOFFMAN  81

Jennie Michel BY AMY HOFFMAN COUTURE  84

84

Adam Van Dusen BY M. J. CODY  88

J. G. Hustler BY AMY HOFFMAN COUTURE  91

P. W. Gillette BY LIISA PENNER  95

Bridget Grant BY NANCY HOFFMAN  98

Cleveland Rockwell BY NANCY HOFFMAN  102

102

Charlotte Smith BY AMY HOFFMAN COUTURE  107

Marshall J. Kinney BY NANCY HOFFMAN  109

Alfred Kinney BY NANCY HOFFMAN  112

Narcissa Kinney BY NANCY HOFFMAN  114

Charles William Fulton BY NANCY HOFFMAN  115

August Erickson BY AMY HOFFMAN COUTURE  118

Jack Williams BY NANCY HOFFMAN  121

118

128

130

141

151

172

202

210

Frank I. Dunbar BY AMY HOFFMAN COUTURE  123

Herman Wise BY JOHN GOODENBERGER  126

John A. Buchanan BY AMY HOFFMAN COUTURE  128

Minnie Hill BY NANCY HOFFMAN  130

Joseph Riippa BY NANCY HOFFMAN  132

Rose Ingleton BY NANCY HOFFMAN  134

Melville T. Wire BY NANCY HOFFMAN  136

Maria Raunio BY M. J. CODY  138

Polly McKean Bell BY NANCY HOFFMAN  141

Sam Schnitzer BY M. J. CODY  143

Anna Bay BY M. J. CODY  147

John E. Wicks BY NANCY HOFFMAN  151

Fritz Elfving BY NANCY HOFFMAN  154

Francis Clay Harley BY LIISA PENNER  158

Lem Dever BY NANCY HOFFMAN  160

David James Ferguson BY JOHN GOODENBERGER  164

May Miller BY JOHN GOODENBERGER  166

Joe Dyer BY M. J. CODY  168

Rolf Klep BY NANCY HOFFMAN  172

Burnby Bell BY M. J. CODY  176

Emil Richard "Dic" Nivala BY NANCY HOFFMAN AND LIISA PENNER  179

Helmi Huttunen Mellin BY LIISA PENNER  183

Edward Harvey BY JOHN GOODENBERGER  187

Edgar Quinn BY NANCY HOFFMAN  189

Sam Churchill BY NANCY HOFFMAN  190

Wally Palmberg BY NANCY HOFFMAN  193

Charles Haddix BY LIISA PENNER  196

Svenson Sisters BY NANCY HOFFMAN  198

Michael Foster BY M. J. CODY  202

Liisa Penner BY M. J. CODY  206

Robert Adams BY M. J. CODY  210

About the Authors  217

Index  219

# Introduction

)(

By Stephen Aldrich Forrester

Editor and Publisher, the *Daily Astorian*

Calvin Trillin in Astoria, October 1992.

By Robin Loznak for the *Daily Astorian*.

Calvin Trillin's voice on the phone was the kind of random, unexpected event that makes life interesting for a small-town newspaper editor. Trillin was reading newspaper clippings about the criminal case of Harry Flavel.

"Is this still going on?" Trillin asked me.

"It will always go on," I replied.

Trillin said he would like to come to Astoria to research an article for the *New Yorker*. I offered him the use of our offices. Our dialogue during his three-week residence in our newsroom was a conversation about Astoria's eccentrics. By the end of his stay, he shared my appreciation for the human comedy of this small town at the mouth of the Columbia River.

I maintained that to be an Astorian is to live among eccentric and extraordinary people. It is as true in 2011 as it was in 1811.

As a young person growing up in Pendleton, I developed a fascination with eccentricity, because these were some of the most interesting people. Our fabled governor, Tom McCall, was the acme of eccentricity—a descendant of New

Rolf Klep, ca. 1970.

England blue blood who grew up among cowboys in Central Oregon. He was a hybrid of those two disparate cultures. His visits to our home during the Pendleton Round-Up were a delight. On one of my first visits to Astoria as a young adult, I accompanied my parents to a Boxing Day party at the Kenneth McAlpin residence. The personalities in the room that evening were out of an English novel. There was McAlpin, the bar pilot, in his Scottish kilt; the always ebullient fish-processing magnate Graham Barbey; and Rolf Klep, whose personal drive and enthusiasm filled the room like a bright light. Klep collected marine artifacts and believed he could create a major maritime museum in a town that was then quiet and economically depressed. By force of will, he made it happen.

Extraordinary people are not necessarily eccentric. But eccentrics are driven to do extraordinary things.

As Portland historian Chet Orloff once said, "There is history on every street corner of Astoria, if you know what you are looking at." To live in Astoria is to be conscious that one is standing on the top layer of an archaeological dig. There are dead bodies underneath us, and we live with the ghosts of the bustling nineteenth-century seaport with sailing ships. That town built on wooden pilings with its saloons, card rooms, and brothels must have been breathtaking. I can imagine the hubbub of the Louvre Saloon, August Erickson's pleasure palace. I feel the excitement of the Ross Opera House.

I suspect that rural places generate more eccentricity than urban places. The storied English eccentrics typically were country people. In trying to explain Tom McCall's outsized character, I concluded that when you live in a place largely empty of human population, your personality expands to fill the void.

Astoria is not rural in the prairie way. But the broad reach of the Columbia River is a raw physical presence. And Astoria was the product of John Jacob Astor's dream. Astorians have not gotten over the romance of Astor's concept. That draws us to this picturesque place.

Barbara Hansel nurtured a keen appreciation for Astoria's eccentrics. As the proprietor of Parnassus Books, she watched the world go by—peering over her reading glasses, hair swept up in a bun, wearing sturdy tweed—while sitting on her stool behind the cash register. Hansel and I frequently talked about the mystery of the town's propensity to cough up such vivid personalities. She had a theory. "In biology, the richest life forms reside at the edge of the ecosystem," she said. "And here we are at the edge."

Drawing of Francis Clay Harley from the *Astoria Budget,* September 4, 1915. COURTESY OF THE ASTORIA PUBLIC LIBRARY.

This book is a celebration of that larger-than-life quality that has appeared with regularity in the town's long history. Here is the notorious Bridget Grant, the hilarious scoundrel Mayor Francis Clay Harley, the elusive English "barmaid" Jane Barnes, and many other characters who left indelible marks on what the psychologist Carl Jung might call the collective unconscious of Astoria.

We are especially grateful to Calvin Trillin for granting us permission to publish "First Family of Astoria" as the opening of this book.

# PART 1

# The Magnificent Flavels

## *First Family of Astoria*

X

### By Calvin Trillin

Y OU CAN'T REALLY TALK about Astoria without talking about the Flavels. It isn't that Astoria's history is so thin that it can be dominated by one family. As visitors are informed at the city limits, Astoria is the "Oldest Settlement West of the Rockies," dating from a post that John Jacob Astor's Pacific Fur Company established a dozen miles from the mouth of the Columbia River in 1811. As early as 1836, Washington Irving wrote an entire book about Astoria, although his inspiration was apparently not the history Astoria had seen but the fee Astor was willing to pay. By then, the fur-trading post had withered and died—not through any fault of John Jacob Astor's, readers were assured by Irving, who wrote, "It is painful, at all times, to see a grand and beneficial stroke of genius fail of its aim." By the later part of the nineteenth century, though, Astoria was thriving, thanks to its proximity to the mouth of the Columbia and to a supply of lumber and salmon that appeared to be inexhaustible.

Finnish and Swedish and Norwegian gill-netters worked the river by boat; horses that were kept in barns built on pilings in the river were brought out on the islands exposed at low tide, to haul in seines. Astoria's waterfront was lined with canneries, where the salmon was processed by a contract-labor force so uniformly Chinese that when an automatic fish-skinner was finally invented it was known as an Iron Chink. Astoria's port was busy sending the product of its lumber mills across the Pacific, and there was also work for its mariners close

---

"American Chronicles: First Family of Astoria" appeared in the *New Yorker* in February 1993. It is reprinted with the kind permission of Calvin Trillin. The footnotes with updates are new to this publication.

LEFT: Mary Christina Flavel, ca. 1854. FLAVEL COLLECTION, CCHS 532.00F.

RIGHT: Captain Flavel, ca. 1855. FLAVEL COLLECTION, CCHS 531.00F.

to home, on the Columbia bar—the shallow passage where a local pilot is taken aboard to deal with the tricky combination of tides and currents and winds brought together by the meeting of the ocean and the river. Throughout all this, Astoria, like any number of small towns in the Pacific Northwest, nurtured grandiose dreams of its destiny. A promotional poster published in 1926 says, under a drawing of the skyscrapers envisioned on the banks of the Columbia, "The Future New York of the Pacific—God's Highway to the Sea."

In the decades beginning around the time of the Civil War, God did not control the Highway to the Sea. The Columbia bar belonged to Captain George Flavel.

One of the earliest bar pilots licensed by the State of Oregon, Flavel managed to put together what amounted to a bar-pilotage cartel. A ship going into or out of the Columbia River had to deal with him, and his rates reflected a keen awareness that options to his services were not readily available. In those days, talk about the Flavels included a lot of talk about the Captain's stranglehold on the bar; an editorial of the times refers to him as "this bloodsucker at the mouth of the river." Still, by the time Captain Flavel died, in 1893, after a business career that had expanded from bar pilotage and shipping to include timber and banking and real estate, one newspaper said, "The death of Captain George Flavel removes from our midst Astoria's most prominent citizen."

A decade before his death, George Flavel had erected an elaborate Victorian mansion, in a style described as Queen Anne or Italianate or Carpenter Gothic, and from there his widow, who had been only fourteen when she married the Captain, presided over Astoria society for thirty years the way Mrs. Astor was said to have presided over society in the New York of the Atlantic. (According to one rather rarefied theory, the Flavels lorded it over the other "pioneer families" of Astoria not simply because of their wealth and prominence but because most of the other families had come overland by wagon instead of arriving by ship.) The Captain's spinster daughters—Miss Nellie, a coloratura soprano, and Miss Katie, an accomplished pianist—lived out their lives in the mansion, although they were often mentioned in the newspapers for having returned from music studies in Europe or having departed to spend the winter season in New York. The Captain's son—also a captain, also

LEFT: Mary Christina Flavel with young son, George C. Flavel, ca. 1857. FLAVEL COLLECTION, CCHS 04.093.048. RIGHT: Captain Flavel, ca. 1870. FLAVEL COLLECTION, CCHS 530.00F.

named George—assumed his father's place among the most prominent citizens of Astoria.

George C. Flavel and his sister Nellie, ca. 1865. Flavel Collection, CCHS 533.00F.

LEFT: Katie Flavel, ca. 1884. RIGHT: George Conrad Flavel, ca. 1875.

FLAVEL COLLECTION, CCHS 4244.00F.

Patricia Flavel, ca. 1932. Patricia inherited the Flavel House from Nellie,
her great-aunt, and gave it to Clatsop County. FLAVEL COLLECTION, CCHS 5670.00F.

The Flavel House at Eighth and Duane Streets, Astoria, ca. 1885. Mary Flavel is seated on the porch; Nellie and Katie are standing in the yard. A servant is on the porch, and Louis, the gardener, is in the yard on the north side. A carriage with driver and two horses is waiting on Eighth Street. SEPIA PRINT. FLAVEL COLLECTION, CCHS 30189.965.

The music room at the Flavel House. FLAVEL COLLECTION, CCHS. COURTESY OF STILL IMAGES.

Mary Christina Flavel's bedroom at the Flavel House.

Flavel Collection, CCHS. Courtesy of Still Images.

Left: The library at the Flavel House. Flavel Collection, CCHS. Courtesy of Still Images.

Right: The dining room at the Flavel House. Flavel Collection, CCHS. Courtesy of Still Images.

The mansion eventually passed into the hands of the Clatsop County Historical Society, which began guided tours and published a booklet devoted to the history of the family. Long before that, the Flavel line had shifted to another mansion: in 1901, the second Captain George Flavel built a less grandiose but extraordinarily handsome frame house of his own several blocks away from where his sisters were holding their musicales. His son—Harry M. Flavel, the grandson of the founder—inherited that house, as well as his father's position as president of the Flavels' bank. The daughters born to Harry M. and his first wife settled in California, but he and his second wife, a schoolteacher named Florence Sherman, started another family, which remained in Astoria. Harry M. Flavel died in 1951. His widow, Florence, is now [1993] in her nineties.

Their children, Mary Louise and Harry Sherman, neither of whom has ever married, are [in 1993] in their sixties. In other words, the current Flavels are

George C. Flavel mansion at Fifteenth and Franklin Streets, ca. 1971. Courtesy of Bill Penner.

Detail of photo showing Harry Melville Flavel (center) at Smith Lake in 1907. CCHS 4212-147.

presumably the last Flavels that Astoria will have available to talk about, and, it has to be said, Astoria has made the most of the opportunity.

Astoria did not become the New York of the Pacific. It reached its high point, of about twenty-five thousand inhabitants, during the Second World War, partly because of the wartime level of activity at a local naval base. The naval base closed, though, and improved dredging of the Columbia pulled a lot of port business upriver, toward Portland. Astoria also began to suffer from the fact that neither salmon nor lumber turned out to have been in limitless supply after all. In Astoria these days, it's still possible to see a gigantic freighter being loaded with hemlock trunks on their way to Japan, but almost all the mills have closed. The waterfront, which once had twenty-two canneries and at least that many saloons, is quiet. The headquarters of Bumble Bee, which had provided the town with what one resident calls "the sort of people who serve on school boards," packed up and moved to San Diego a dozen years ago. The great ethnic neighborhoods—the Finns in Uniontown, the Swedes and Norwegians in Uppertown—have largely broken up, through intermarriage and the departure of the young to follow the job market.

People who still live in Astoria tend to look back with some longing to the days when there was work for any able-bodied young man who wasn't afraid of it, but they also tend to accept the hand they've been dealt. They are often described as stoic, a characteristic associated with the dark countries in the northernmost part of Europe and with people who work hard in industries based on elements that seem beyond anyone's control—the number of fish in the river, say, or the amount of lumber needed by some faraway country nobody has ever been to. Astoria remains a place strongly marked by its history. It has a working waterfront, even if there hasn't been much work lately, and streets full of splendid Victorian houses that rise from downtown in a way that is likely to reward a casual glance out the kitchen window with a magnificent view of the river and a couple of freighters and the hills of Washington state on the northern bank. In recent years, a sprinkling of outsiders, some of them drawn by the Victorian houses and the history, have settled in Astoria. Still, it remains less than half the size it once was—that rare example of an Oregon coastal town that has lost population.

There is agreement in Astoria that the Flavel family has also been in decline. Some say that it was in Harry M.'s time that the family's performance began to fall behind its prominence. Although Harry M. Flavel is remembered as a charming man, he was not the civic heavyweight that his father and grandfather had been. ("What he had to give was different than what they gave to this community," an Astoria editor said at the time of his death. "He gave cheerful self-effacement, a warm and gentle honesty that the world needs much of these days.") He apparently did not overwork after the family bank was acquired by a larger bank. Even before Harry M. Flavel died, there was talk about erratic and angry behavior by his son, Harry S. One summer evening in 1947, when the younger Harry was only twenty, a man named Fred Fulton, who lived next door to the Flavels in a nearby beach community, heard Florence Flavel shouting for help. Fulton rushed into the Flavel house, broke through an upstairs hall door to free Mrs. Flavel, and then, trying to break into the bedroom to which young Harry had fled, was cut on the arm with a hatchet. At Harry's trial for assault with a dangerous weapon, the Flavels agreed, according to the local paper, that Mrs. Flavel had been in no danger, her son having locked her into her room simply so she could concentrate on finding a key that was important to him. ("The son considered the evening of June 5, 1947, as good a time as any for having her look for it, the youth's testimony established.") Harry Flavel, arguing that he had used the hatchet in self-defense, said that he had been frightened by a strange look on Fulton's face; Florence and Mary Louise Flavel said that Fulton was surely drunk. Young Flavel was found not guilty, but for a while he was known to some as Hatchet Harry.

*Young Flavel was found not guilty, but for a while he was known to some as Hatchet Harry.*

He turned out to have an aptitude for matters scientific and mechanical, which came in handy for maintaining the commercial property the family still owned in downtown Astoria—basically, two buildings, on Ninth and Commercial, with eight or nine storefronts that were rented for years to such substantial enterprises as a bank and the local power-company office. No one

Mary Louise Flavel (at left) with brother Harry Sherman Flavel and
mother Florence Flavel in 1961. Flavel Collection, CCHS 889.00F.

doubted Harry's intelligence—he seemed to soak up knowledge, not just from
books but also from unlikely sources, like tool catalogues or the sides of shipping cartons—but he had an intensity that often made people uneasy. "Harry
would go along all right for a while," a lifelong Astoria resident has said, "and
then something would set him off."

Mary Louise Flavel, who was more sociable than her brother, and always
made a fine first impression, seemed to have inherited the family interest in
music. She was active in the local concert series, which would have made her
Great-Aunt Nellie and her Great-Aunt Katie proud, except that the best-known
stories about the family participation became stories about how the Flavels had
promised to underwrite one of the concerts and then reneged or stories about

the night that the police came to haul Mary Louise Flavel off to jail because she refused to leave a Community Concert reception she had not been invited to. For some years in the sixties, she spent most of her time in New York; according to the talk in Astoria, she had become friendly with Jerome Hines, the Metropolitan basso, and, maybe with his help, had become a manager of opera singers. But she returned in the early seventies, full of stories about the New York opera world, which some people in town said they'd take with a grain of salt, and she moved back with her mother and her brother in the imposing house her grandfather had built.

From then on, it was common to see at least two of the three surviving Flavels together. Florence Flavel and her daughter were regular worshippers at the Presbyterian church, which had been built largely through the beneficence of the Flavel family. Mary Louise and Harry would usually appear together when there was business to go over with their downtown tenants. A tenant who had just had a visit of an hour or two with Harry and Mary Louise would sometimes discover that their mother had been waiting outside in the car the entire time. As the years passed, the Flavels seemed close to the exclusion of other people. Florence and Mary Louise might call on a neighbor for tea, but the neighbor did not return the visit. Although strangers were shown daily through the ornate mansion built by the original Captain, it became unusual for anybody at all to enter the house in which Flavels were living.

The absence of eyewitness reports about the imposing Flavel residence, of course, only increased curiosity about what might be found inside. In Astoria, winters are long and dark; because it isn't exactly on the way to any place, it has an atmosphere of isolation that enriches local legend. A lot of people who live in Astoria have been there a long time—long enough to respond to a Finnish name, for instance, with stories of how the Finns of Uniontown were considered clannish and dangerously left-wing, long enough to have traded legends about how ships owned by old Captain Flavel's competitors seemed to experience bad luck, if that's what it was. One prominent citizen believes that, in the way some places are called City of Churches, and Portland, a couple of hours to the south-east, is called the Rose City, Astoria could be called City of Rumors. A place the size of Astoria is likely to have at least one rather reclusive family living in a large house, but it isn't normally the first family of the town. Since before the

Civil War, the Flavels had been the subject of a lot of talk in Astoria—talk about the old Captain's scheme to establish a town called Flavel, say, or about his son's purchase of Astoria's first motorcar, or about his grandson's divorce—and the talk didn't stop simply because there was no longer a Flavel at the bank.

There were some known facts. It was clear, for instance, that the Flavels adopted stray dogs. It was clear that Harry's angry shouting could sometimes be heard by neighbors and passersby. But a lot of stories about the Flavels tended to have more than one version. Maybe Harry used the bannister in the Flavels' house for firewood and maybe he chopped it up with his hatchet just to irritate his mother or sister and maybe it wasn't a hatchet but a chain saw and maybe the bannister was removed for some perfectly sensible reason that nobody happens to know. Maybe Mary Louise returned from New York because she ran out of her share of the Flavel estate and maybe because her only client was stolen by another agency and maybe because her father (who died fifteen years or so before this version could have taken place) went to New York and found her starving herself to death in a luxurious Park Avenue apartment. Maybe when Florence and Mary Louise Flavel wanted to go on a trip around the world that Harry was said to oppose they left secretly by cab after Harry dropped them off at church and maybe they secretly borrowed a car and left it in the Park 'n' Fly at the Portland airport.

*❧ What people agree on was that the Flavels were difficult to deal with. "Difficult?" a local businessman said not long ago. "Impossible!" ☙*

There was consistent talk in Astoria about Harry and Mary Louise Flavel showing up in the dark of night in the premises of businesses that rented space in their buildings on Commercial Street. Some people thought they had extra keys; some people preferred to think that they appeared, as burglars sometimes appear in Astoria, through abandoned streets that became basement-level tunnels when the old downtown burned in the twenties and the new downtown was built right on top of it. What people agree on was that the Flavels were, for some of their tenants and other Astorians they came in contact with, difficult to deal with. "Difficult?" a local businessman said not long ago. "Impossible!" A woman who once had to negotiate with the Flavels in a meeting having to do with a historical-society matter—a meeting that seemed dominated by Mary Louise Flavel's concern that the family was not being given its due—has said, "It was the longest three hours of my life, and I count major surgery and childbirth."

Some businesspeople in Astoria gave the Flavels a wide berth because they had a reputation for being litigious. One retailer, a woman who came to Astoria from a different part of the country, recalls being impressed by Mary Louise Flavel while looking for a suitable space for her store ("She talked about being an impresario in New York. I thought she was smart, interesting"), and then, after choosing another space, being told she would be hearing from the Flavels' lawyer about breach of a verbal contract. As it turned out, the retailer was not sued, but there are businesspeople in Astoria who would swear that she's the only one. The Flavels were not always the plaintiffs. At one point, the hotel at the Portland airport got a judgment against Mary Louise Flavel—the contention was that she and her mother had maintained a room there for some months and had not paid for it—and when lawyers tried to attach Flavel property in Astoria there was a flurry of countersuits. Merchants traded stories about goods delivered on approval or loan that were hard to get back. Nobody knew whether the Flavels had a shortage of money or a disinclination to spend it, but it was known that they were not easy people to collect a bill from. For one thing, the collectors couldn't get in the door. Kandy Renninger, the only private process-server in Astoria, says that the first time she successfully served Harry Flavel, a lawyer who had no involvement in the dispute stopped her on the street half an hour later to congratulate her.

All this might have been made more irritating to the residents of Astoria by the fact that the Flavels—particularly Mary Louise Flavel—seemed to have an air appropriate for people who still controlled the bar pilotage and the bank and a good part of downtown. Even after the huge house seemed somewhat neglected and Mary Louise Flavel's wardrobe seemed to have narrowed, she retained a rather grand manner. "Mary Louise seems almost aristocratic," a man who has dealt with her in Astoria said recently. "Once, I had a long conversation with her, and only at the very end did I notice that the lining of her coat was hanging loose. It was not apparent at first, because of her bearing." Some residents of Astoria didn't mind her manner—she was not really arrogant—but some residents felt that they were being condescended to by someone whose house needed painting.

Mary Louise Flavel has always had her defenders in Astoria. There are people who believe, for instance, that she should have been invited to that Community Concert reception—she had been an effective member of the society—and that the fault lay not with her but with a high-handed chairman. An older resident who has known her all her life said not long ago, "Mary Louise is a nice girl, just as normal as she could be—well, a little eccentric with her renters." One of the theories about the eccentricity of the Flavel family is that Florence and Mary Louise grew strange trying to cope with Harry, or that they were in thrall to Harry, either because he was physically menacing to them or because he may have somehow ended up with the Flavel money. But there are also people in Astoria who believe that Mary Louise is the most difficult member of the family, particularly when it comes to business.

What seemed to bother a lot of people in Astoria about the Flavels was that their way of doing business—never settling for the hand they were dealt—often worked. According to the stories, a merchant might take back a somewhat used item rather than cause an argument or a lawsuit. Although people who are difficult to collect from may have trouble getting credit, they may also end up paying less. "They seemed to get a thrill out of getting the better of people," one resident of Astoria said not long ago. "They had a miraculous way of coming out on top." As the years passed and the Flavels got a bit more reclusive and, in the minds of some Astorians, quite a bit more irritating, a lot of the talk about Astoria's first family was not about how much they had done for the town but how much they seemed to get away with. Then, in 1983, Harry Flavel got involved in an incident that it seemed unlikely he was going to be able to come out of on top. It involved a young man named Alec Josephson.

Alec Josephson's forebears were Northern Europeans who made their living from salmon. His maternal grandparents spoke Finnish at home. His father's father was a Swedish gillnetter. In February of 1983, when the encounter with Harry Flavel took place, Alec Josephson was twenty-two years old and had recently married; a former captain of the high-school basketball team, he was taking some community-college courses and hoping, as he put it, to "go into the Army and jump out of airplanes." On the evening in question, he had watched a Portland Trail Blazers game on television with some friends and shared a pitcher or two of beer with them at the Workers Tavern, in Uniontown; at around ten-thirty, he was on his way home when he was startled by a noise that made him think his car had been hit by a rock. Enraged, Josephson stopped his car—this was on Irving Street, a residential street about ten blocks above the river—and went looking for what he assumed would prove to be kids up to no good.

He found Harry Flavel—in a dark walkway next to the gymnasium of the Roman Catholic school, Star of the Sea. Flavel had been out walking two dogs and had thought that Josephson was travelling too fast. Apparently, the noise Josephson had heard was Flavel's chain dog leash being swung at the car. There were some angry words. Hearing an argument from his room in the rectory nearby, Father Arthur Dernbach called the police. A couple of minutes later, after going down to see for himself what was happening, Father Dernbach phoned again, to say that an ambulance would be needed: the one man who remained there, next to the gym, had been stabbed. From what the emergency-room surgeon said later, Father Dernbach's intervention saved Alec Josephson's life. Josephson had lost a lot of blood. A blade had come within half an inch of passing completely through his body—entering at the stomach and nicking the nerves near his spine at the back.

*❧ Father Dernbach's intervention saved Alec Josephson's life. A blade had come within half an inch of passing completely through his body. ❧*

The police showed up at the Flavels' pretty quickly. Josephson had been able to say that the man who stabbed him was an older man who had been walking two dogs, and a neighbor knew who routinely walked his dogs on that stretch of Irving Street every night. But talking to Harry Flavel about the events of the evening turned out to be a problem. Nobody had ever had an easy time getting into the Flavels' house, and the police who showed up to ask him about the stabbing of Alec Josephson were no exception. As the police and the District

Attorney, Steven Gerttula, stood on the front porch, the Flavels talked to the city manager on the telephone. (They had phoned the city manager, Harry Flavel later testified, because they knew that the police chief was out of town, leaving in charge an officer who had not long before refused Flavel's request to help him make a citizen's arrest of a tenant, and had done what Flavel called "nasty little things to me and my family.") Flavel turned himself in a couple of days later, and the police eventually got a warrant to search the Flavel house for a weapon. But there was muttering in Astoria that Harry Flavel had once again been allowed to get away with something.

Flavel was charged with attempted murder and first-degree assault, which in Oregon is assault that involves using a deadly weapon with an intent to do serious injury. He pleaded not guilty, insisting that he had acted completely in self-defense against someone he referred to as a "madman." In a pre-trial hearing, Flavel's attorney, a well-known Portland criminal lawyer named Des Connall, managed to get a ruling that would have admitted a lie-detector test that he considered supportive of Flavel's version of events. By the time that ruling was reversed and a few more postponements were granted, more than two years had passed. Alec Josephson was just about fully recovered—the nick in the nerves near his spine having caused a slight weakness that lingered in one leg. In the spring of 1985, Harry Flavel finally came to trial, in St. Helens, the seat of the adjoining county. A change of venue had been granted after a hearing in which an assistant of Connall's who had taken a telephone survey among potential jurors in Clatsop County testified that she had not received a single positive response to a question about Harry Flavel's general reputation, and that many of the times she had recorded a "no opinion" it was because "when I would ask the question I would get a lot of laughs."

It was a particularly contentious trial. It lasted more than two weeks, and it wasn't difficult for those attending to get the impression that Des Connall was reluctant to let a day pass without a motion for a mistrial. Connall and Glenn Faber, the deputy district attorney who tried the case, were constantly embroiled in bitterly contested matters of procedure and admissibility of evidence. The defense spent an extraordinary amount of time trying to prove that Josephson had consumed more than the half-dozen beers he acknowledged having had during that long evening, and the prosecution, in addition to presenting evidence to contradict that contention, argued that the effort to portray Josephson as drunk was simply an attempt to find some way of making Harry Flavel's story believable. Flavel testified, more or less as he had testified forty years before in his trial for assaulting his next-door neighbor with a hatchet, that he had acted completely in self-defense, trying to calm down a young man who seemed drunk or "drug-crazed" or somehow deranged. According to Flavel's testimony, Josephson, constantly threatening to kill him, had come at him perhaps a dozen times, swaying before him between attacks with a strange look on his face. Flavel said that even after he took out his pocketknife and waved it threateningly Josephson tried to choke him, and would have surely killed him if the knife hadn't been used.

The prosecution argued that it was absurd to believe that the tiny Boy Scout knife Flavel carried had inflicted the wound that the attending surgeon described as having reminded him of a bayonet wound. Josephson, acknowledging that he had shouted at Flavel angrily and called him a "fucking jerk," testified that the only time he had touched Flavel was when he grabbed him in order to keep him from leaving before he had given his name and address. The prosecution presented some circumstantial evidence that argued against Flavel's version of events—the angle and size of the wound, for instance, and Flavel's behavior after the stabbing—but basically the jury had to decide whether to believe Harry Flavel or Alec Josephson, the only two people who knew for certain what had happened behind the Star of the Sea gym that night. The jury found Harry Flavel not guilty of attempted murder but guilty of first-degree assault.

In Oregon at the time, a trial judge automatically handed down the statutory sentence for a crime—up to twenty years for first-degree assault—and then turned the defendant over to a state board, which would decide the actual time to be served. Under the guidelines then in place, Flavel would probably have done two or three years. But the judge, after imposing the customary sentence, suspended it, and gave Flavel five years' probation, on the condition that he pay restitution to Josephson for medical expenses and serve a year in the county jail. Flavel was certainly going to appeal the guilty verdict—even before the sentencing, his lawyers had moved for a new trial—and Des Connall told the judge, in open court, that the trial had contained so many errors of law that the verdict would obviously be overturned on appeal. The judge agreed that the year in jail would not have to be served until the appeals process had been exhausted. There are those in Astoria who believe that he did not understand what "exhausting the appeals process" would mean to the Flavels.

Harry Flavel's strongest ground for appeal had been discovered by a defense lawyer among the medical bills handed in for restitution: when Josephson's recovery seemed to be going more slowly than it should, he had undergone nearly a dozen sessions of "hypnotherapy," administered by a mental-health counselor whose only degree, it turned out, was a certificate in mortuary science. Because of the delay in starting the trial, this had been well before Josephson took the stand, and the defense pointed out that it had not been carried out according to state rules designed to prevent the enhancing of a witness's memory through hypnosis—rules that in Oregon include the videotaping of all sessions. That argument was rejected without comment by the Oregon Supreme Court, and so were a number of others. The defense turned to the federal system, and managed to take the case all the way up to the Supreme Court of the United States twice, also without success. The way people in Astoria tended to see it, the Flavels were using their money—which seemed to be there when they needed it, despite their reputation for thriftiness—to try to get away with something yet again. As the appeals worked their way through the courts in the years following Harry Flavel's conviction, it was often said in Astoria that Harry Flavel would never see the inside of a jail.

During the appeals process, Mary Louise Flavel tried some more direct approaches: she would show up, unannounced, at the door of an appeals-court judge or an influential public official, making her usual excellent first impression, and stay the evening, presenting her argument that the entire case was simply a malicious witch-hunt. That didn't work, either. Apparently, there was some hope among defense lawyers that, even if the appeals did not succeed, the passing of time and the cooling down of community concern about the incident might induce the judge to drop the condition of probation which called for Harry Flavel, a reclusive man in his sixties, to spend a year in jail. But that didn't happen. Finally, in August 1990, the court accepted Glenn Faber's argument that all appeals had been exhausted. The lead paragraph of the account in the *Daily Astorian* summed up the judge's order in four words: "Go directly to jail."

By that point, though, the defense had a new argument. Five years had passed since the sentence was handed down. During that period, Harry Flavel had reported to his probation officer regularly; he had just turned over to the court the final payment for restitutions. Defense lawyers argued that, the assigned probationary term having been served, the judge no longer had any jurisdiction over Harry Flavel. The judge responded by extending the probation for a year to make time for the jail term; the defense appealed his right to make that extension; and, just before Harry Flavel was due to turn himself over to the sheriff, a higher court stayed the jailing so that it could consider the appeal. But there were two new problems. One was that Mary Louise Flavel had stopped payment on the final restitution check. The other was that Harry Flavel was nowhere to be found. Neither was his sister. Neither was their mother. Neither were their two dogs. The Flavels, people in Astoria said, were on the lam.

*Some people in Astoria wondered whether going from motel room to motel room in a gang that included a ninety-two-year-old woman and two dogs was really preferable to going to jail for a year in Astoria.*

For two months, there was no word of the Flavels. Then, toward the end of October 1990, Harry Flavel turned up in jail in Montgomery County, Pennsylvania. Apparently, there had been a question about whether the Flavels had removed some towels from their room at a motel in Willow Grove, outside Philadelphia, and a check of their license plate turned up the information that Harry Flavel was wanted in Oregon. An extradition order was granted, but Flavel, to the surprise of no one in Astoria, contested it. On New Year's Eve of 1990, with the argument over extradition still in progress, he was released from jail on payment of a fifty-thousand-dollar cash bond. After some delays having to do with which lawyer would represent him, a hearing was set for March 5, 1991, at the Montgomery County Courthouse. Harry Flavel did not appear. The Flavels were off again. Some people in Astoria wondered

*Harry at Home,* © 1991 and 2010 by R. Doane Hoag, is on the cover of this book.

whether going from motel room to motel room in a gang that included a ninety-two-year-old woman and two dogs was really preferable to going to jail for a year in Astoria. In the words of one resident, "it couldn't have been much like Thelma and Louise."

In November 1991, fifteen months or so after the Flavels had left Astoria, a maintenance man at the Residence Inn in Tewksbury, Massachusetts, not far from Boston, became suspicious about a family that had been in residence a long time. It isn't unusual for people to stay awhile at the Residence Inn, which is designed more like an apartment complex than a motel; it's sometimes used by people in training programs for nearby high-tech industries and by executives who have been transferred to the area and are still house-hunting. The family in question, though, didn't fit either of those profiles, and they paid their bills in cash. The maintenance man, who was a former police officer, checked their license plate, and not long after that a couple of F.B.I. agents showed up at the door to arrest Harry Flavel. Three months later, after a number of delays and appeals, a Boston judge ruled that Flavel had to return to Oregon. Three months after that, on June 8, 1992, Harry Flavel was finally in the Clatsop County jail, awaiting a hearing at which the court would decide whether to revoke his probation. The *Daily Astorian* began its story, "Harry Flavel is back in town."

By that time, some people in Astoria—particularly the sort of people who are interested in the history and the Victorian houses—had begun to look on Harry Flavel's case with a certain amount of amusement. At the Ricciardi Gallery, where customers can order espresso and latte, in the Pacific Northwest manner, and linger over copies of *The New York Times,* in the New York manner, a steady stream of citizens came by to have a look at a painting of a younger man standing in the window of a house that looks just like the house that Harry and Mary Louise and Florence Flavel lived in. Its title is *Harry at Home.* Among the coffee drinkers, there was a certain amount of speculation about what being on the lam with the Flavels might have been like and how long the saga of Harry Flavel's criminal case could last. "I love the Hitchcock element," one resident said not long ago. "I love the story that their house seemed so haunted that when the police did the search for the weapon policemen with loaded guns were afraid to go down to the basement. It's like having a caricature of a first family."

Shortly after her son's arrest, Florence Flavel fell seriously ill, and she is on a respirator in a hospital not far from Tewksbury.* There has been talk in Astoria that Mary Louise Flavel was living in sordid conditions in some tiny motel room, but in fact she is living in the same neat two-bedroom unit at

---

*Florence S. Flavel, born on March 1, 1896, died on February 1, 1994, in Worcester, Massachusetts.

the Residence Inn that the family was in when her brother was picked up. She remains well spoken and courteous—a rather handsome gray-haired woman, gracious in the way someone in the leading family of a town might be gracious; so that in recounting a story, say, she might remark with approval that someone had a strong handshake or seemed to have been properly brought up. She still likes to talk about her days as a manager of opera singers; among the keepsakes

Mary Louise Flavel (right) and Lucia Evangelista Hines greet the basso Jerome Hines after his La Scala debut as Hercules. COURTESY OF *OPERA NEWS*, FEBRUARY 2, 1959.

she has with her is a copy of a full-page ad in *Musical America* with a portrait of the tenor Flavanio Labo and a notation that exclusive management is by Mary Louise Flavel. In those days, she says, Rudolf Bing had such faith in her judgment of young singers that when she recommended a young baritone to the Metropolitan Bing offered him a contract without troubling to hear him sing.

James Sardos, who has been Jerome Hines' manager for thirty years, rolls his eyes at the story about Bing, but he says that Mary Louise Flavel did manage Flavanio Labo, a small but mighty Italian tenor, and "through a kind of innocent persistence" got him back into the Metropolitan after his contract had been dropped. Sardos remembers her as a fan—an opera fan and, particularly, a fan of Jerome Hines—who eventually got into the business, and didn't do badly at it for a few years, handling Labo and perhaps a few other singers. Jerome Hines, who, at seventy-one, is still giving concerts, agrees."* He says that she had indeed grown close to him and his family at one time—in 1955, she became godmother to his first son—but that contact with her grew faint after she moved back to Astoria. The last time the Hineses saw her, he says, was when she showed up at their place in New Jersey in December of 1990. Among the topics she wanted to discuss was whether Hines could be of some help in raising fifty thousand dollars to bail her brother out of jail in Pennsylvania. He couldn't.

Mary Louise Flavel says that, whatever people in Astoria may believe about her reasons for giving up her career as a manager of opera singers, she returned to Astoria simply because her mother needed help with the management of the downtown property, her brother's interest being in the maintenance end rather than the business end. Without becoming angry or defensive, she can dismiss all the Astoria versions of the stories about the Flavel family—even versions supported by a number of eyewitnesses—and replace them with versions that show the family to be at least innocent and probably put upon. A lot of her stories involve someone who seemed nice at first but turned out not to be—that next-door neighbor who got cut with a hatchet in 1947, for instance, who, she says, chose to believe that Florence Flavel was crying out for help when she was actually having an allergic reaction to some medicine. Mary Louise Flavel does not accept the proposition that the Flavels were ever on the lam. They had been

---

*Jerome Hines died February 4, 2003, after singing forty-one seasons at the Metropolitan Opera.

forced to remain in Astoria for the five years of her brother's probation, she says, and when that ended they took a trip. She speaks of it the way her Aunt Nellie or her Aunt Katie might have spoken of a motor tour of the West or a visit to New York during the winter season.

They first went to Denver, she says, because "my former next-door neighbor, a young actress, was living in Denver and she had wanted me to come visit her." But Florence Flavel, her daughter says, suffered from the altitude in Denver, so the family headed south, and proceeded to the East Coast along a route that was close to sea level. In Mary Louise Flavel's telling of the tale, the three-thousand-mile journey across the country is much more slowly paced than *Thelma and Louise*: quiet mornings when Florence Flavel preferred to rest instead of moving to the next destination; rather leisurely days in the car, with regular stops to walk their two dogs, Odin II and Dugan; a week's stay in Virginia when Florence Flavel got pneumonia.

And where were they headed? To Philadelphia, she says, where Dr. Martin T. Orne, an expert on the effects of hypnosis on court testimony, happens to live.* Apparently, they never actually saw Dr. Orne, although Mary Louise Flavel says that she paid a visit to his house and had a nice conversation with his wife. Then, after a stop in New York—she had been hoping to ask the advice of a lawyer she knew when she lived in the city, she says, but he turned out to have died—they came to the Residence Inn, which they chose because of its proximity to the Boston area and its welcoming attitude toward their dogs

Why the Boston area? Dershowitz. According to Miss Flavel, her brother had read the books of Alan Dershowitz, the Harvard Law School professor who has handled a number of high-profile appeals, and believed that Dershowitz had the experience and the intelligence to get the original conviction overturned. She says that they attended some of Dershowitz's lectures ("fascinating, very interesting") and tried to pin him down for an appointment, to no avail. "We had at least three appointments," she says. "But something more important always came up—I mean from his point of view." On the day her brother was taken to jail in Boston, Mary Louise Flavel says, "I immediately went to

---

*Dr. Orne, a native of Vienna and longtime professor of psychiatry and psychology at the University of Pennsylvania, died in 2000.

Professor Dershowitz's house to tell him that it was an emergency. He lives in Cambridge, just a block from the governor. Beautiful residential area." She says that Dershowitz, about to leave for California, suggested another lawyer, but that the recommended lawyer had a secretary who turned out to be "haughty." In fighting her brother's extradition to Oregon, she also tried the direct approach that she had used in Oregon: apparently, she knows how close Dershowitz lives to the governor because she approached the governor, both at a ceremony in downtown Boston and at home. But her stories of such efforts tend to begin with the person in question giving the impression of being a trustworthy and open person but sooner or later "turning cold."

Mary Louise Flavel sees the prosecution of her brother as a miscarriage of justice that has been aided by "untrue, inflammatory, prejudicial" press coverage. One of the letters she sent Dershowitz was written on a copy of an article from the Portland *Oregonian* that she had color-coded, so that yellow highlighting indicated material she believes is contradicted by the trial transcripts and pink highlighting indicated material—a story, for instance, about Harry's locking her and her mother out on the balcony that wraps around part of the second story of their house and spraying them with a garden hose—that she categorizes as "maliciously fabricated and false." She often quotes third parties—a woman who quietly approached her at the supermarket in Astoria to say that Harry was being railroaded; a veterinarian who said that one of the Flavels' dogs might have been poisoned—to bolster her contention that her family has been persecuted. She has at times accused Steven Gerttula, the District Attorney, of being a cousin of Alec Josephson, on the Finnish side of the Josephson family, and both she and her brother sometimes see his prosecution as a vendetta that can be traced to some of the run-ins the Flavels have had with the city and the county and the police. But she also talks about a less specific animus in Astoria against the Flavel family.

*But sometimes we meet people and they hate us. They don't know why and we don't know why. Something having to do with their grandfather and grandmother—things we know nothing about.*

"Sometimes, we meet people and they like us because one of their ancestors worked for Captain Flavel and was well treated," she has said. "But sometimes we meet people and they hate us. They don't know why and we don't know why. Something having to do with their grandfather and grandmother—things we know nothing about."

It would be difficult to find anybody in Astoria who believes that what has happened to Harry Flavel is the result of any sort of vendetta. "For Harry, the whole world's out of step and he's in step," someone who has known the Flavels for years said recently, expressing a sentiment that is often heard in Astoria. "He's above the law. Everything's unfair, he could have taken his medicine and saved himself a couple of hundred thousand." Still, as one resident put it not long after Flavel's return, "the District Attorney's office is obviously not unhappy about seeing Harry Flavel get his comeuppance. These people have just been so irritating."

Steven Gerttula, who says he is not related to Alec Josephson, believes that the problem is that Harry Flavel has been treated not too harshly but too leniently, beginning with the original sentence of probation rather than prison and the judge's willingness to postpone the jail term even then. People who worked on the prosecution side tend to think that the trial judge was overimpressed by the self-assurance of a big-shot Portland defense lawyer. (Since Flavel says that his counsel absolutely assured him that he would be acquitted, and then absolutely assured him that the conviction would be overturned, he might have been overimpressed by the self-assurance of a big-shot Portland defense lawyer himself.) The unfortunate impression given by the Flavel case, Gerttula believes, is that someone with enough money—and Flavel's willingness to walk away from a fifty-thousand-dollar bond in Pennsylvania convinced a lot of people in Astoria that he had enough money—can subvert the legal system.

> *The unfortunate impression given by the Flavel case is that someone with enough money can subvert the legal system.*

In recent months, both Gerttula and Glenn Faber have left the Clatsop County District Attorney's office for private practice. The position of the county is still that Flavel's probation should be revoked—meaning that he would serve a penitentiary term, presumably minus the time that he has already spent in jail—but, eight months after Harry Flavel got back to town, the hearing to decide that has not been held. The judge recently recused himself. Flavel, not for the first time, has been between lawyers. At this point, the case of *Oregon v. Harry Sherman Flavel* seems becalmed, but that is not to say that the Flavels have exhausted the appeals process. Reminded not long ago that no appeals court has ever ruled on Flavel's contention that the judge lost jurisdiction over him after the five years of probation were over—a contention some lawyers think of as perhaps audacious but not necessarily without merit—Gerttula just smiled and nodded.

Harry Flavel is sixty-five now [in 1993]—an intense man, with longish gray hair and a jailhouse pallor. He still seems to be the sort of man who might be described, as he has been described by a longtime acquaintance, as "always on the edge." He still seems to be the sort of man who might be described, as he is often described in Astoria, as terrifically smart—practically a genius, some say, in matters mechanical. (According to one story in Astoria, Flavel completely took apart the boiler of his house, but the story then splits into the customary two versions on the question of whether he managed to get it back together.) When he meets with a visitor, he takes copious notes on yellow legal pads, even if the visitor is an old friend just trying to buck up his spirits, and he's alert to anything he considers a misstatement. A visitor who begins a sentence by saying "If you believe you are innocent" will be interrupted instantly and almost angrily: "I don't believe I am innocent. I know I am innocent."

These days, Flavel is not easily diverted from the subject of his case. He is conversant not only with the events of that night—he still insists that Josephson was drunk or high on drugs or disoriented by steroids or badly affected by the movie *The Warriors,* which had come on just after the Trail Blazers game, or in a "self-induced psychosis"—but also with areas of law having to do with, say, special conditions of probation and the effect of hypnosis on testimony. Flipping furiously through the pages of his legal pad, he'll cite an Oregon regulation or a case out of North Carolina. He says that the jury consisted of "unsophisticated people from a semi-rural area who didn't understand the concept of self-defense and didn't reach a just verdict." Far from believing that he has subverted the legal system, he insists that it is his right—his duty, really—to appeal an unjust verdict. ("I believed that the system had self-correcting factors built in. I fully expected to have it correct its errors.") He sees himself as the true victim: "I went to trial and I told the truth and this is what happened to me."

The complaints that Harry Flavel is getting away with something are not quite as pointed now that he will have to file his appeals from the Clatsop County Jail. Counting the time in Pennsylvania and Massachusetts, he has already served much more than a year. He has, according to his sister, exhausted his inheritance on legal fees. He has spent months as a fugitive—although he wouldn't acknowledge that he was a fugitive. ("When I left the state of Oregon, I was a free man. The judge acted illegally. He had no jurisdiction.") The rest of his family—and the Flavels, of course, have always been a close family—are at the other end of the continent. An outsider might expect to find in Astoria a body of sentiment for calling a halt to the whole business and letting Harry Flavel go home.

*"I really felt some sympathy for him. I thought, This thing has really cost him. Then he started haranguing the judge. I thought, Now I remember this guy. It all came back."*

Steven Gerttula says that he has not heard those feelings expressed—quite the opposite—and other people who circulate widely in the community agree that Astoria simply doesn't have much sympathy for Harry Flavel. Asked why, both of the Flavels are likely to mention a saying about Russians that in their view works equally well for Finns: Nothing makes them happier than the misfortune of their neighbor. The Flavels, of course, have no capital of goodwill to draw on. In the words of one businessman, "They haven't exactly been lovable over the years." In addition to everything else, downtown people often mention the family's neglect of its commercial real estate, which now consists of facing lines of nearly empty storefronts. Lately, there has been some discussion about whether the tourism industry, properly developed, might be an answer to Astoria's economic problems. The area already has, among

The Flavel house on Fifteenth Street in 2010. By Alex Pajunas for the *Daily Astorian*.

other attractions, a fine maritime museum and a monument to Lewis and Clark, and a tour through the mansion that was built by Captain George Flavel. The last thing the town boosters want is the appearance of near abandonment on an important downtown corner.

Harry Flavel may have been slowed down some by the events of the past several years, but he hasn't lost his capacity to irritate. "When they brought him back here and he came into court, he looked so much older and tireder," one of the people who had worked on the prosecution said recently. "I really felt some sympathy for him. I thought, This thing has really cost him. Then he started haranguing the judge. I thought, Now I remember this guy. It all came back."

Not long ago, one resident said that, however much Astorians complain about the Flavels, they feed on the family's story, and would hate to see it end. If Astoria is to be the City of Rumors, he points out, it has to have prominent people to spread rumors about, and in recent years the cast has been thinning. Even if the Flavels are a caricature of a first family, they are the only first family that

Astoria has. Mary Louise Flavel would not put it that way, but her interpretation of the events of the last several years sometimes seems close to that. "If our name were not Flavel, in Astoria," she said, "this would not be happening to us."

Some years ago, John Goodenberger gave a public performance as
Captain George S. Flavel. For the occasion, Mary Louise Flavel gave him
the tailcoat her father wore at his wedding in 1908. In a nice turn of living
history, her father was the same size as Captain Flavel, and so is
John Goodenberger. In 2006, on the hundred and fifth anniversary
of Captain Flavel's death, Goodenberger again portrayed Flavel in a
reenactment of his lying in state in the parlor of the Flavel Mansion.
LaRee Johnson donned a nineteenth-century mourning dress
and veil and paid her respects to the deceased Captain.
COURTESY OF THE *DAILY ASTORIAN*.

# Epilogue, 2010

### BY JOHN GOODENBERGER

In 1992 Harry Flavel was extradited back to Astoria, where he served time at the Clatsop County Jail. If anyone asked, he would tell them his stay exceeded his sentence, and the fact that he served more than a year was proof the courts were out to get him. Once released, Harry returned to Tewksbury, Massachusetts. There he rejoined his sister, Mary Louise. His mother, Florence, died soon afterward; she had been on life support in a Worcester, Massachusetts, hospital for two years.

The siblings' reclusive nature became more so. In fact, when they returned to live in Oregon, no one knew it. When Mary Louise checked in with her Astoria commercial tenants, townspeople went into shock akin to that of having seen a film star—wide-eyed, slack-jawed, "I've seen her!"

Harry, of course, was rarely spotted. He remained convinced that a large arm of the local criminal justice system was bound and determined to find any excuse to throw him in jail. "My attorney once told me," he said, "that my treatment by the local police department was worse than Stalag." Therefore, Harry chose to avoid the courts and the curious. He remained in the car while Mary Louise took care of the family business.

As time passed, Flavel "sightings" became less frequent. Neighbors might see them coming or going from their crumbling, boarded-up mansion, but the Flavels rarely stayed long to talk. Their visits were fleeting. Like an apparition, the Flavels simply faded away.

# Other Notable Astorians

## Coboway

X

### By M. J. Cody

*Ocian in view! Oh! the joy.*
>—Captain William Clark, November 7, 1805

L ewis and Clark and the men of the Corps of Discovery were elated when they caught the first glimpse of their destination. No one could foresee the consequences of their journey across the continent. For some it would mean paradise found; for others, paradise lost. Coboway, the chief of the Clatsop Indians, befriended and provided for Lewis and Clark at a pivotal intersection in history.

The Corps' arrival in their homeland must have been curious indeed for Coboway and the coastal tribes. These pah-shish-e-ooks, or "cloth men," came from the wrong direction—from the east, downriver, rather than from the sea—and at the wrong time of year, as trading vessels arrived only in spring and summer, never broaching the angry sea or crossing the treacherous Columbia River bar in winter. The intruders had little of trading value, nothing like the bounty the tribes encountered in their dealings with the ships that plied northwestern waters. The Clatsops and the Chinooks, their brethren across the Columbia River to the north, were accustomed to the ships' visits and were skilled traders. Their economic and social network stretched for hundreds of miles along the coast and inland along the Columbia River to the eastern plateaus.

Photographic image from a 2004 painting by Roger McKay, showing a
Clatsop longhouse and canoes. CCHS HERITAGE MUSEUM.

The Corps built their winter quarters on the banks of the Netul River (now
named the Lewis and Clark River) in Coboway's domain, which stretched from
Point Adams at the mouth of the Columbia River as far south as Arch Cape and
east from Smith Point on Youngs Bay to the summit of Nehalem Mountain.
Coboway's principal village, "the place of pounded salmon," was located at what
is now Fort Stevens. According to Clark's journal, Coboway's village consisted
of eight "long houses" made of cedar planks, which sheltered perhaps a hundred
Indians.

On December 12, 1805, Clark noted a visit from Chief Coboway, who
brought gifts of roots and berries. This is the first documented encounter, though
it was probably not their first meeting: "Those Indians appear well disposed we
gave a Medal to the principal Chief named Con-ny-au or Com mo-wol and
treated those with him with as much attention as we could."

Throughout their winter stay at Fort Clatsop, Lewis and Clark traded with
the chief they referred to as "Con-ny-au," "Conia," or "Com mo-wol." According
to the chief's great-great-great grandson, Richard Basch, who lives in Seaside,

Oregon, and is currently the American Indian Liaison for the Lewis and Clark National Historic Trail, the accurate name is Coboway.

It is regrettable that so little was recorded about Coboway. He was, in Clark's words, "much the most friendly and decent savage that we have met with in this neighbourhood."

No physical description of Coboway has come down to us. He must have had the flattened forehead common to royalty of the Chinook and Clatsop people, known as "Flatheads." The term referred to the Indians' sloping foreheads, a result of pressing a slab of wood or bark across an infant's brow and binding it tightly to the cradleboard.

No doubt Coboway had several wives. The exact number is unknown, but his father had twenty wives. Chiefs were esteemed in proportion to their possessions—dugout canoes, slaves (captured from other tribes), and wives—as well as their generosity in giving to the poor and hosting celebratory "potlatch" feasts. The Clatsops believed in guardian spirits, which resided in animals and in inanimate natural objects. They were great gamblers and were "certainly the best Canoe navigaters I ever Saw," according to corpsman Patrick Gass. Coboway may have been, like his tribesmen, "naked except for the small robes which hardly cover their shoulders" and barefoot most of the year. In winter, the Clatsops wore cedar cloaks, sealskin robes, and rain hats woven of cedar and grasses.

A Chinook cradle used for head-flattening. From *A History of Oregon* by Robert Carlton Clark, Robert H. Down, and George V. Blue, Chicago and New York: Row, Peterson and Company, 1926, p. 17. PENNER COLLECTION, CCHS.

Photographic image from a 2004 painting by Roger McKay illustrating the seasonal round of life of the Clatsop Indians. The berry-picker at front left has a flattened forehead and carries a baby in a head-flattening cradleboard. CCHS Heritage Museum.

Coboway often visited Fort Clatsop and sometimes stayed overnight. He brought gifts and trade items such as salmon, roots, berries, seal and otter skins, dogs (a culinary delicacy for the Corps), anchovies, watertight cedar-bark hats, and blubber from a beached whale. In turn, Coboway received Shoshone tobacco, fishhooks, a razor, a moccasin awl and thread, and a pair of satin breeches that "much pleases" him, in the words of Captain Lewis.

Lewis and Clark disdained the social structures and the rules of trade of the "troublesome savages," an intricate pursuit that could last hours or days and sometimes involved ceremonies with games, dances, and offerings to the spirits. Lewis wrote that the Clatsops were "great higlers in trade," and an exasperated Clark wrote, "I can readily discover that they are close deelers, and Stickle for a very little, never cl[o]se a bargain except they think they have the advantage."

The Corps redefined Clatsop territory. They drew boundaries and constructed walls with sentries at guard posts, declaring the shores of the Netul near the fort off limits to the Indians. Coboway took these affronts in stride and continued to visit the fort.

In February 1806, George Drouillard, a hunter and interpreter with the Corps, shot seven elk and cached them to retrieve later. Lewis wrote that he was "apprehensive that the Clatsops . . . will rob us of a part if not the whole of it." The meat was stolen, but after a complaint to Coboway, the thief was dispatched to make amends. Lewis wrote: "This morning we were visited by a Clatsop man who brought with him three dogs as a remuneration for the Elk which himself and nation had stolen from us some little time since, however the dogs took the alarm and ran off." Drouillard retrieved the dogs in the Indian village and returned them to the awaiting cooking pots.

The "dreadfull weather" brought snow, sleet, and unrelenting rain. Game was scarce, and provisions at the fort were depleted. Many corpsmen were ill with fever. Though Coboway maintained friendly relations and prevented an Indian attack on Fort Clatsop, Lewis railed against the "savages," warning his men to be vigilant against "the well known treachery of the natives."

*Though Coboway prevented an Indian attack on Fort Clatsop, Lewis railed against the "savages," warning his men to be vigilant against "the well known treachery of the natives."*

As the Corps undertook preparations for their homeward journey in 1806, the treachery of Lewis and Clark proved to be the low moral point of the expedition. The Corps needed two more canoes, but the Clatsops refused to sell. Not only did a canoe provide transportation essential to Clatsop livelihood, but it held much power. It was revered, a thing of beauty and spirit, as well as a coffin that guided the dead to the next world. A canoe was worth a wife, and not to be bargained for lightly.

According to Lewis, Drouillard finally procured an "indifferent" canoe from the Chinooks. Considering the Corps' need for transportation more important than Clatsop tradition, Lewis wrote, "We yet want another canoe, and as the Clatsops will not sell us one at a price which we can afford to give we will take one from them in lue of the six Elk which they stole from us in the winter."

The Corps of Discovery stole a Clatsop canoe, wrote corpsman John Ordway, "as we were in want of it." In recompense, Lewis and Clark gave Coboway "a certificate of his good conduct and the friendly intercourse which he has maintained with us during our residence at this place; we also gave him a list of our names."

On March 23, 1806, the Corps of Discovery left Fort Clatsop. The previous evening Lewis wrote: "To this Chief [Coboway] we left our houses and fu[r]niture. he has been much more kind an[d] hospitable to us than any other indian in this neighbourhood."

Chief Tostum, nephew of Coboway, ca. 1865. Oregon Historical Society, OrHi-CN4326.

Left: Silas B. Smith. By A. B. Paxton, Astoria, ca. 1890. Depping Collection, CCHS.

Right: Kate Juhrs, daughter of Chief Tostum and grand-niece of Coboway, ca. 1910.

CCHS 23933.00J.

The Clatsops used the fort infrequently for a few years as a seasonal hunting hut. But it was, as Richard Basch points out, "a sorry shelter compared to their own. The roofs slanted inward toward the courtyard, accumulating rain into permanent mud puddles." It was likely used merely for overnight accommodation in inclement weather.

Historical records offer no further mention of Coboway until December 1813. Alexander Henry, a trader with the North West Company, noted that Coboway arrived to sell salmon and elk and that "the old Clatsop chief" made several visits to the newly established Fort George thereafter. Eventually, Coboway showed Henry the document Lewis and Clark had given him—a prized possession he had kept intact in the damp climate for nearly eight years. After a theft at Fort George, Coboway, conciliatory as usual, returned the stolen goods. Henry expressed gratitude but asked to see the Lewis and Clark document again. When Coboway obliged, Henry crumpled it up and threw it into the fire. Henry gave Coboway a new document declaring that Astoria was the possession of England, not America.

The cruel act must have been heartbreaking, yet clear to Coboway: he was no longer sovereign in his realm. At the stroke of a pen, these cloth men could decree new rules and new nations. Coboway apparently understood the consequences. As chief, it was his duty to arrange his daughters' marriage to men in positions of power. Coboway saw to it that his three daughters were married, not to neighboring chiefs, but to white men.

Coboway died in 1824. He did not live to see his clansmen killed and his village destroyed in 1829 by Hudson's Bay Company men, a misbegotten tragedy; he did not see the decimation of his people by European diseases; nor did he witness, thanks to an unratified treaty, the invasion of white settlers, who by 1852 occupied nearly all his homeland.

Coboway's second daughter, Celiast, and her husband, Solomon Smith, carried on his even-tempered and generous legacy. Both Celiast and Solomon were revered as conciliatory agents between the white settlers and the Clatsops. Smith was elected state senator, and their son, Silas, became a renowned attorney brokering treaties between the states and indigenous people.

# Donald McTavish

X

## By Amy Hoffman Couture

The mouth of the Columbia River is known as the Graveyard of the Pacific because so many seaworthy vessels have crossed oceans, weathered storms, and visited ports around the world, only to wreck in the turbulent waters near Astoria. Since the early part of the nineteenth century, approximately seven hundred people have lost their lives near the mouth of the Columbia River. Donald McTavish was one of the first casualties.

McTavish was born in a small village in Stirlingshire, Scotland, about 1771. His cousin Simon McTavish was a high-ranking employee of the North West Fur Company in Montreal, and Donald was hired as an apprentice clerk with the same company when he was about nineteen. Soon he led Canadian

Astoria in 1811. From a publication by G. P. Putnam's Sons. CCHS 511-900.

wilderness expeditions to establish fur-trading contacts with Indians in what are today Saskatchewan and Alberta. McTavish became a partner in the company when he was about twenty-eight, taking charge of a fort on Canada's English River, northwest of Lake Superior. In the winter of 1811–1812, near age forty, McTavish bought a Scottish estate near his childhood home, apparently looking forward to his upcoming retirement. When spring came, he returned to Canada to assist the North West Company in its plans to establish itself strategically in the Oregon Country and initiate direct trade with China.

With the onset of the War of 1812, the Americans of John Jacob Astor's Pacific Fur Company recognized they would be no match for the British Navy and decided to sell Fort Astoria to the Canadian North West Company. A Scottish relative of McTavish's and fellow North West Fur Company employee, John George McTavish, negotiated the sale of the fort for $58,000 in October 1813. Meanwhile, because of "his known integrity" (as his partners in the North West Fur Company affirmed), Donald McTavish had been appointed by the company to lead the expedition of the *Isaac Todd* and a British naval frigate from England to Astoria, in order to formally take possession of the fort from the Americans. Upon their arrival, McTavish was to serve as Chief Factor, or governor of the fort.

In March 1813 in Portsmouth, England, as McTavish prepared for the voyage to Astoria with John McDonald, his second in command, he officially witnessed a written agreement between McDonald and the English barmaid Jane Barnes. In the agreement and in exchange for an annual salary, Barnes agreed to accompany McDonald to "do any needle work that may be necessary" on board the ship. Their contract apparently ended in Rio de Janeiro, when McDonald left the *Isaac Todd* for the faster naval ship. McTavish took over as Barnes' companion for the remainder of the voyage. The *Isaac Todd* reached Astoria (now renamed Fort George by the Canadians and British) in April 1814. Initially, McTavish was protective of Barnes. But the fort clerk, Alexander Henry, soon became her new companion, and McTavish developed an amorous relationship with a Chinook woman.

> *Barnes agreed to accompany McDonald to "do any needle work that may be necessary" on board the ship.*

For about a month, McTavish was extremely busy with his duties as the head of the fort. Henry's journal entries indicate that McTavish made frequent trips upriver and across the river to meet with Chinook and Clatsop leaders. Then, on a stormy day in May 1814, McTavish attempted to row from the *Isaac Todd* back to shore. His open boat capsized, and along with five others (including Alexander Henry), McTavish drowned.

North West Fur Company employees buried him near the fort, at what is now the intersection of Seventeenth and Exchange Streets in Astoria. About seventy years later, as road crews constructed Exchange Street, they uncovered old coffins and skeletons that may have included McTavish's remains. The engraved stone that once marked his grave is preserved at the Clatsop County Historical Society. The inscription reads, "In Memory of D. McTavish, Aged 42 Years, Drowned Crossing This River, May 22, 1814."

The headstone of Donald McTavish in 2009. CCHS 83.015.001.006.

# Jane Barnes

## )(

### By Amy Hoffman Couture

In the spring of 1814, forty-nine male clerks and indentured servants and a handful of Indian women and children were isolated at rainy, forest-bound Fort George (the former Astoria, a fur-trading outpost on the site of modern Astoria). They were unaware that a beautiful female visitor was approaching by sea, and her presence would soon create turmoil in the social dynamics of the fort.

Jane Barnes, a young British woman described as "flaxen-haired [and] blue-eyed," crossed the Columbia River bar on April 17, 1814, the first white woman to set foot on the shores of the river. Her adventure had begun thirteen months earlier at a hotel pub in Portsmouth, England, where she worked as a waitress. At her workplace, she was known for her charismatic debates with men about gender roles and Shakespeare's portrayal of women. Two customers, Donald McTavish and John McDonald, were making final preparations for their trans-oceanic voyage to the outpost at the mouth of the Columbia in order to take possession of the fort from the Americans, who had sold it to the Montreal-backed North West Company. McTavish was to represent the company as the new governor at Fort George, and McDonald was to oversee the military take-over of the fort. The two men apparently intended to travel in comfort and had packed cheese, bottled beer, and "prime tinned English beef." They were impressed with Barnes at the pub and, perhaps to increase their comfort level on the journey, invited her to travel to the Pacific Northwest aboard their ship, the *Isaac Todd*. In a written agreement, Barnes accepted the offer to "do any needle work that may be necessary on the passage" in return for an annual salary of "thirty pounds sterling" and all "necessary articles of clothing suitable for the country." After several days of shopping for new dresses in Portsmouth, Barnes left England aboard the *Isaac Todd* on March 25, 1813. Because of the threat of American aggression during the War of 1812, the well-armed British naval ship *Raccoon* accompanied the *Isaac Todd*.

Jane Barnes

Articles of Agreement entered upon before witness, between Mr. John McDonald for himself and on behalf of the North West Company on this one part and Miss Jane Barnes of Portsmouth on the other part— The said Jane Barnes consents to do any needle work that may be necessary on the passage and elsewhere when nothing happens to prevent such.

The said John McDonald for himself and the North West Company binds and obliges himself to pay or cause to be paid the sum of Thirty pounds sterling yearly to the foresaid Jane Barnes and every necessary articles of clothing suitable for the Country, in consideration of the above services or one half at the expiration of every six months should she require the same—he further binds himself that her treatment shall be as good as circumstances will admit and to procure her a passage home when suitable to both parties.

Portsmouth 17 March 1813

J. McDonald

In presence of Mr. McTavish

J. C. McTavish

Witness

Text from *The Oregon Country under the Union Jack: A Reference Book of Historical Documents for Scholars and Historians,* ed. B. C. Payette, Montreal, Canada: Payette Radio Limited, 1962, p. 636.

Historical sources are unclear about the nature of the relationships between Barnes, McDonald, and McTavish while en route to Fort George. But in Rio de Janeiro, McDonald switched to the faster HMS *Raccoon,* and McTavish continued the journey with Barnes. The young woman's presence apparently generated

Image from the *Illustrated London News,* February 10, 1849.
The caption reads as follows: "On Fort George, or Astoria, Columbia River—Site of the Hudson's Bay Company's Establishment." CCHS 33854.906.

rivalries among the crew, and the ship's captain was relieved when his ship finally entered the Columbia River.

By the time the *Isaac Todd* arrived at Fort George, a clerk named Alexander Henry noted that Barnes was definitely McTavish's "mistress." Within weeks, however, Henry's diary entries suggested he spent a significant amount of his own time with Barnes. By May 8, Henry had arranged a comfortable living space for Barnes in the fort, and she left the *Isaac Todd* without McTavish. Meanwhile, McTavish married a Chinook woman in the custom of the country but showed signs of jealousy over the new arrangement between Barnes and Henry.

*Within weeks, however, Henry's diary entries suggested he spent a significant amount of his own time with Barnes.*

After only a month at Fort George, Barnes' circumstances changed again, when McTavish and Henry both drowned after their open boat overturned in high swells on the Columbia. The fort's physician, Dr. Swan, apparently took Henry's place as Barnes' companion, and Barnes remained at Fort George throughout the summer.

Local tavern workers compete for the title of Jane Barnes in an annual contest, ca. 1990.
*Daily Astorian* Collection, CCHS.

Walking along the river beach below the fort each evening in her fashionable European dresses, she attracted the attention of Chinook chief Comcomly's son Cassakas. The British agents at the fort had a volatile relationship with Comcomly and his Chinook confederation and worried about Barnes' potential role as their ambassador. Three times, Cassakas appeared at the fort dressed in his formal native attire and proposed marriage to Barnes, but she politely refused. Cassakas angrily said that as long as Barnes was at the fort, he would "never more come there." The new governor, James Keith, became aware of a plot among Cassakas' friends to kidnap Barnes and was eager to send her back to England. She left Fort George on August 16, 1814, probably aboard the schooner which was bound for England by way of Alaska, Hawaii, and China.

While in China, Barnes met and married a British employee of the East India Company. It appears that she continued her sea-going adventures with her new husband and two young children for several more years. Clerks at the fort reported that Barnes, again dressed in the latest fashions from Europe, made a second visit to Fort George in 1818.

# Robert Shortess

ᛉ

## By Amy Hoffman Couture

I n 1903, startled construction workers discovered the unmarked grave of a
woman just east of Astoria in Alderbrook. Upon investigation, state historians identified the remains as those of Robert Shortess's wife, a Clatsop Indian
who committed suicide around 1850. The grave was on property that was once a
part of Robert Shortess's donation land claim. In 1846, after a long wait for land
of his own, he claimed the 320 acres between John Adair's land on the east end
of Astoria and Henry Marlin's claim at Tongue Point.

Shortess was born March 3, 1797, in Pennsylvania. When he was a young
adult, his family moved west to the
Ohio frontier. Like many other pioneers,
Shortess believed that acquisition of
land was vital for survival. An older
brother was set to inherit his family's
land, so Shortess decided to head westward. In the late 1830s he was in central Missouri, traveling alone and on
foot beside the Osage River, when he
stopped to talk with a stranger, Lindsay
Applegate. In need of a miller for his
newly constructed grist mill, Applegate
hired Shortess, and the two men began
a friendship that lasted many years. Still
eager to own his own land, Shortess
joined the Oregon-bound Peoria Party
(also called the Oregon Dragoons) in
Independence, Missouri, in 1839. They
followed the Santa Fe Trail as far as Fort

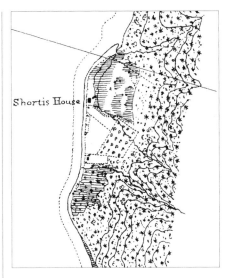

Detail of an 1868 U.S. Coast Survey
map by Cleveland Rockwell, showing
the house and claim of Robert Shortess,
in the area now known as Alderbrook.
By the Pacific Northwest River Basins
Commission. CCHS Collection.

59

The Whitman Mission's station at Waillatpu. From *How Marcus Whitman Saved Oregon* by Oliver W. Nixon, Chicago: Star Publishing Company, 1895. CCHS 91.034.002.

Bent. Internal conflict caused the party to break apart; at least two smaller parties proceeded separately to Oregon.

Shortess and his party traveled from fort to fort across present-day Colorado, Wyoming, Montana, and Idaho in the fall of 1839. As winter approached, the other members of the group turned back or chose to spend the winter at the trapping forts along the way. Shortess continued his journey toward Oregon, leaving Fort Hall, near present-day Pocatello, Idaho, with a single companion. They navigated over snow-covered mountains until they finally reached Fort Walla Walla and the Whitman Mission in early December.

Shortess spent the winter with the Whitmans then left for the Willamette Valley in March 1840. When the scattered remnants of the Peoria Party finally arrived in the Willamette Valley in 1839 and 1840, they were termed part of the "Great Reinforcement" because so few white settlers were in Oregon at the time.

The Hudson's Bay Company was powerful in Oregon Country in 1840, and Shortess was an outspoken opponent of the company's monopoly of local industry. Methodist, anti-British, and loyal to the United States, he participated at the Champoeg public meeting in 1843, when Oregon settlers voted to form a provisional government with ties to the United States. Shortess described Oregon's opportunities and mild climate in letters to his former employer Lindsay Applegate, convincing Applegate and his extended family to emigrate to Oregon from Missouri. The Applegate clan joined one of the first wagon trains to Oregon. After three Applegates died in the rapids near Celilo Falls, the family blazed the "Applegate Trail," a southern route into the Willamette Valley that avoided the dangers of the Columbia River,

By 1846, Shortess was settled on his Alderbrook land claim. He soon became a teacher and Indian sub-agent. He married a Clatsop Indian named Ann, and they had a daughter, Susan. When his friend Calvin Tibbets died of cholera while on board the trading schooner *Skipanon* in 1849, Shortess became guardian of Tibbets' two children, John and Grace. When his own daughter was about four years old, Ann Shortess took her own life. Historical records do not reveal the circumstances of her death, but we know that as Indian sub-agent, Shortess attempted to limit the Clatsop Indians' access to alcohol. During the nineteenth century, alcohol consumption by Indians had extremely detrimental social effects, and suicide was not uncommon. It is possible that Shortess's strong prohibition against alcohol was a direct result of Ann's suicide. Shortess never remarried, but raised his daughter and the two Tibbets children on his own. Disillusioned by his dealings with the state's department of Indian affairs, Shortess resigned from his role as a sub-agent in 1851.

Superintendent
Indian Affairs
Ogn Territory
Astoria, May 17th 1851

Dear Sir:

With Surprise and mortification I have learned (unofficially) that the Board of Commissioners is dissolved & we are to have no meeting of the Indians at this place for treaty purposes. Consequently, I am placed in the disagreeable condition of being considered as having made statements not founded on facts, and encouraged false hopes in the natives of this sub agency. In view of this and various other reasons, I respectfully decline any longer acting as sub agent, or being in any manner connected with the Indian department in Oregon.

Please inform me when and where it will be convenient to settle up my accounts as sub agent.

With the highest regard, and feelings of the warmest personal friendship

I subscribe myself


Your Humble Servt.

R. Shortess

---

Text from microfilm of Robert Shortess letters, Oregon Historical Society Collection. PHOTOCOPIES AT CCHS.


Early in the morning of April 8, 1854, Shortess was on board the *Gazelle,* a Willamette River steamboat that was docked near Oregon City with about sixty passengers and crew. The engineer's negligence caused a sudden and violent explosion of the ship's two boilers. Twenty-four people died in the explosion, and Shortess was among twenty-five injured.

In the early 1860s, Shortess was superintendent of the Astoria schools. He earned a good salary and was respected in the community. By 1870, however, he could not pay a $600 debt and gave up the deed to most of his land. Hubert H. Bancroft, author of the 1886 two-volume *History of Oregon,* wrote that Shortess then lived "as a recluse" until he died in Astoria in 1878.

# John McClure

X

By Amy Hoffman Couture

The present location of the Clatsop County Courthouse on Commercial Street between Seventh and Eighth is the result of a competition between three industrious pioneers in the 1840s. Three of Astoria's earliest settlers—John McClure, John Shively, and Albert E. Wilson—drew land claims on the north slope of the peninsula that is now the city of Astoria. Each platted a city grid on his claim and hoped that his creation would become the focal point of the growing city. After a series of strategic land donations and sales, John McClure's original land claim became the site of Astoria's central business district.

The first of eight children of an Irish immigrant father and an American mother, John McClure was born in Jefferson, Kentucky, in 1788. When McClure was fourteen, his family relocated to Knox County, Indiana, in what was then the Northwest Territory. His experience as an early pioneer in a region recently opened to settlers may have inspired McClure's interest in community planning. It appears that McClure left Indiana in 1839 after the death of his wife, leaving his son and daughter in the care of his mother and an unmarried sister, Caroline.

ASTORIA—FROM CAPT. HUSTLER'S MAP—1870

Drawing of early Astoria, 1870. CCHS 1254.900.

```
                    P A T E N T

UNITED STATES OF AMERICA         Vol. "C" of Deeds, page 209

        -TO-                     Dated March 27th, 1866

JOHN McCLURE, and               Recorded July 17th, 1868
LOUISA McCLURE, his wife


Certificate 1634
Notification 7862
Claim 40

        The claim of John McClure and his wife Louisa McClure has
been established to a donation of ½ section or 320 acres of land,
and that the same has been surveyed and designated as Claim No. 40;
being parts of Sections 7, 8, 17 and 18 in T. 8. N. R. 9. W., acc-
ording to the official plat of survey returned to the General Land
Office by the Surveyor General, being bounded and described as fol-
lows, to-wit:
        Beinning at a point 2 chains and 13 links East of the North
West corner of the North East quarter of said sections 18 and run-
ning thence South 18 chains and 45 links; thence East 65 chains and
90 links; thence North 41 chains and 70 links; thence North 60 de-
grees West 22 chains; thence North 85 degrees West 25 chains; thence
South68 degrees West 23 chains and 80 links, and thence South 27
chains and 39 links to the place of beginning, in the district of
lands, subject to sale at Oregon City, Oregon, containing 334.43
acres.
        Unto the said John McClure and to his heirs, the North half
and unto his wife, the said Louisa McClure, and to her heirs, the
South half of the tract of land above described.

                (Signed)   By the President,
                              ANDREW JOHNSON
                        By Edw. D. Niell, Secretary
        (no seal)            I. N. Granger,
                              Recorder of the General Land
                                        Office
```

Donation land claim description of John McClure's property, from an 1866 title abstract.

CCHS 99.065.001.

Historical records next place McClure in New Orleans, where he worked as a customs officer for a short time before leaving, perhaps under a cloud. From Louisiana, he traveled up the Mississippi River to St. Louis and joined a wagon train traveling west to California along the Santa Fe Trail in 1841. From Los Angeles, McClure traveled overland to Oregon, arriving in spring 1843. After a stop at Fort Vancouver, he paddled a canoe to the small settlement at the mouth of the Columbia and became one of only four white settlers on the land that would become Astoria.

In January 1844, McClure staked a claim of 334 acres in accordance with the Donation Land Act. At this time, the Oregon Country was not yet a territory of the United States or of any other country; a provisional government authorized land grants for settlers. McClure's claim, known as "McClure's Astoria" or "Lower Town," formed a rectangle between today's First through Thirteenth Streets. McClure himself lived in a cabin near what is now Twelfth and Exchange. Because his land included Hudson Bay Company property, McClure was soon involved in boundary disputes with Alexander Lattie, the resident company employee. From his post at Fort George, Lattie wrote in his journal that McClure was an "agitator and one of the worst kind" who was "quite in a boiling heat about the Boundary question." Tensions between the two men grew until they erupted in a violent fist fight, after which McClure was charged with attempted murder.

The 1850 census for Clatsop County indicates that McClure was a relatively wealthy land speculator. While most Astoria residents of the period owned real estate valued at less than $3,000, McClure's real-estate holdings were worth $30,000 ($500,000 in today's market). Adding to his status as a landholder and landlord, McClure was elected to the new Clatsop County government

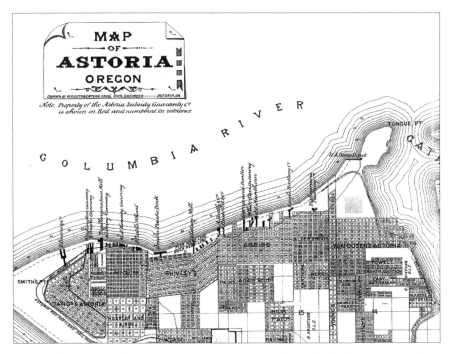

Map of donation land claims in the Astoria area, drawn by W. H. Cuthbertson, ca. 1899.

CCHS COLLECTION.

and became directly involved with developing the community. By 1851, he had served as justice of the peace and county legislator. When county officials decided to move the Clatsop County seat from Lexington (today's Warrenton) to Astoria in 1854, McClure donated two acres of his land for the site of the county buildings, and voters accepted his offer. Over the next decade, McClure gradually sold parts of his land to business and community developers. In the best-known transaction, he sold a fourth of his holdings to Cyrus Olney on February 4, 1858.

The last historical traces of John McClure indicate that in 1851, at age sixty-three, he married a local native woman named Louisa, who may have been one of Chinook leader Comcomly's daughters. Catholic Church records indicate that McClure and Louisa had a son named John or Jean Archibald Concomlly McClure. In 1858, however, McClure left Clatsop County without Louisa and returned to Indiana with their son John. By this time his daughter was thirty-one years old and married, with five children. His first son may have died of tuberculosis.

McClure died in 1861 and was buried near Vincennes, Indiana. Twenty years later, Astoria's McClure School, an elementary and secondary school, was built on his former property and named for him.

# Alexander Lattie

)(

## By Amy Hoffman Couture

While head of the Hudson's Bay Company's post at Fort George, Astoria, in 1846, Alexander Lattie kept a daily journal. His entries described Chinook traders who crossed the river in their dugout canoes, the scurry for land claims among American settlers, and ships that waited several days until it was safe to cross the Columbia River bar. Lattie's journal reveals his wit and sarcasm, giving readers an uncommon glimpse into the mind and personality of a mid–nineteenth century fur trader.

Astoria in 1842. CCHS 297.900B.

In 1830, as a newly employed seaman with the Hudson's Bay Company, Lattie left his hometown of St. Andrews, Scotland, at age twenty-eight. He arrived at Fort Vancouver in summer 1831. The same year, he married a native woman named Marie Catherine Sikkas under the current Hudson's Bay Company laws, and they started a family. By the time their marriage was made official by a Catholic priest, Father Peter DeVos, in 1845, they had five children ranging in age from three to thirteen.

Lattie received training from the native bar pilot "Indian George" and served as the first white river pilot for Hudson's Bay Company ships between the mouth of the Columbia and Fort Vancouver from 1831 until 1846. He lived with his wife and children at Chinook Point and piloted the *Columbia, Cadboro,* and *Beaver* on the Columbia River. Late in 1845, when James Birnie retired from his position as head of Fort George, Lattie took his place as post manager and moved with his family into the fort.

Lattie's well-written journal of his time at Fort George shows that he was a literate man at a time when many of his peers, as well as his wife, were illiterate.

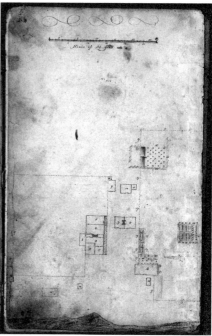

Left: Sikkas, Alexander Lattie's wife, ca. 1860. CCHS 4620.00L.

Right: Sketch of buildings, fields, and gardens for the Hudson's Bay Company at Astoria, by Alexander Lattie. From the Lattie Journal, CCHS 1623.001.

He had a personal library of at least sixty books, including works of classic and contemporary philosophy; histories of Greece, Rome, and England; geographies of Africa, Asia, and the Americas; and technical books about seafaring and navigation. He enjoyed evening conversation with friends such as his predecessor as post manager, James Birnie, and neighbors, Mr. and Mrs. Trask.

Lattie's journal entries also show that he grew frustrated with the American developers in the area, especially John McClure. As Americans drew claims on land that encompassed and bordered Fort George, conflicts arose. On May 13, 1846, Lattie noted sarcastically, "The American friends I have behind me are busy building and clearing." The next day he referred to the same people as "the intruders that are behind me" and warned them about their "impudence." On May 20 he mentioned that his "Boston friends" near the post were "busy raising their rabel [*sic*]," and on May 30 he described his notorious fist fight with McClure in a long entry. Apparently, after hearing McClure's "most awful language," Lattie goaded him by saying, "Colonel, would you like to have the chopping off of one of the [company officers'] heads?" Later, according to Lattie, McClure's anger intensified after a skirmish with Lattie's wife Sikkas, and he fired stray bullets toward the company buildings. Knowing that he and his wife were out of the range of McClure, who was "ramming down a second charge in his riffle [*sic*]," Lattie walked outside and yelled to him "jestingly, 'Ram well, Colenol [*sic*].'"

Although he continued to clash with McClure and other American pioneers and developers, Lattie worked at Fort George for three more years. During this period, a letter to his employer in 1847 indicated that excessive drinking threatened his career. Lattie begged to be "again receiv[ed] in the service" and promised that he would "renounce the use of spirits for the rest of [his] life." Apparently Lattie's alcohol problem continued, however, because he drowned near the mouth of the Willamette River in September 1849 after poling a canoe while intoxicated.

Sikkas lived until 1868 and raised four of her children to adulthood on a land claim in what is now Seaside, Oregon. The many descendants of Lattie and Sikkas now live in Astoria and Seaside and throughout the Pacific Northwest.

# John Shively

)(

## By Nancy Hoffman

You may not know the name John Shively, but if you've driven through Astoria, you're familiar with one of his legacies. Take Duane, Exchange, Irving, or other cross-streets, and you will be forced to make a serious jog between Twelfth and Fourteenth. This is Shively's jog. When John Shively and John McClure platted their sections of the town in the mid 1800s—Shively to the east and McClure to the west—they disagreed on lot size. As a result, the two sections of the town do not line up, and Astorians have been subjected to Shively's jog ever since.

Portrait of John Shively, ca. 1870. CCHS 4008.00S.

Shively was born in Kentucky in 1804. He explored several careers as a young man, including teaching, operating a dry-goods store, and surveying. He married Martha Ann Johnson in 1836, and their son Charles was born in 1839. Martha died in childbirth in 1842. Shortly after her death, Shively left his son with his sister and made his first trip to Oregon. He started from Missouri with a party of 120 wagons and 560 people, but the group broke apart during the journey, and he arrived at Fort Vancouver with few other people.

In January 1844, Dr. John McLoughlin, an officer at the fort, advised him to travel by canoe to Astoria and deal for a land claim. Thus John Shively became one of Astoria's original pioneers. He constructed a log cabin and began surveying the area until he was rudely ousted by representatives of the Hudson's Bay Company. In April 1845, he traveled east on the Oregon Trail to St. Louis and then to Washington, D.C., where he lobbied for mail service to Oregon and published a guide for people traveling across the country: *Route and Distances to Oregon and California with a Description of Watering Places, Crossings, Dangerous Indians, etc.* (Wm. Green, Printer: Washington, D.C., 1846). While in the east, he married Susan Elliott.

In 1847, Shively and his second wife gathered up their belongings, his son Charles, and a shipment of U.S. mail and headed overland to Oregon. He had been commissioned to deliver mail for the United States government and to set up a post office in Astoria. Shively established a post office on the first floor of his home on March 9, 1847, making Astoria the site of the first official U.S. Post Office west of the Rockies.

What happened next remains fuzzy. John Adair, who arrived in Astoria in 1848 and became the local customs officer, claimed to postal authorities that Shively was struck by gold fever in 1849 and dropped everything to travel to California and stake a claim, abandoning his post. Adair took the opportunity to move the post office to "Adairville" on the east side of Astoria, where he maintained the customs office. Shively argued that he had traveled to San Francisco to purchase a steam engine in order to build a transportation link between Portland and Astoria. He discovered that the steam engine would cost $30,000 instead of the $800 he had with him, so he traveled to the gold fields to secure more money. Unfortunately, he lost everything when the ship in which he was returning capsized. Shively later traveled to the gold fields of Jacksonville, Oregon, where he gained as much as $50,000 from prospecting. In Astoria, his fortune continued to grow along with the city.

In August 1856, Shively became the talk of Astoria when Susan filed for a divorce. By that time, they had two children, Cyrus and Joseph, and lived

John Shively operated the first U.S. Post Office west of the Rockies in this house, built by Ezra Fisher, Baptist minister, in the 1840s. Photo ca. 1900. CCHS 171.710.

in a house in downtown Astoria. The divorce was rancorous. Susan charged John with "the harshest and most cruel character." She said he had called her names, forced her to live in poverty, removed the household furniture and her personal clothing, and engaged in acts of intemperance involving the children. Shively countered every claim with a strong denial and blamed their problems on Susan's sister Olivia, who lived with them. He asked for a change of venue, claiming that the judge, Cyrus Olney, was prejudiced against him. The change of venue was denied and the divorce granted in July 1857. Despite the strong words and bitter divorce, the couple remarried two years later.

Upon their deaths, John and Susan were buried separately, Susan with her children and John alone. This suggests that factors other than love—economics, security, or social constraints—may have triggered the couple's remarriage.

Shively's children with Susan died young. One succumbed to tuberculosis, and the other was swept off a boat on the way to art school in San Francisco. Susan died in 1883 and left the bulk of her estate to Astoria's Grace Episcopal Church.

In 1891, Shively, ailing and living in a convalescent home, signed over most of his estate to his son Charles, who lived in Portland with a wife and several daughters. One of the daughters later attended the 1947 centennial celebration of the first post office west of the Rockies. John Shively died in Astoria in 1893.

# Solomon and Celiast Smith

X

## By Amy Hoffman Couture

Solomon Smith, a prominent early pioneer on Clatsop Plains, helped create the Clatsop County government, headed the first school, and later became a state senator representing northwest Oregon. Local landmark Smith Lake testifies to his importance in the history of Clatsop County, but he might never have settled in the area were it not for the influence of his Indian wife, Celiast (Helen).

Solomon H. Smith and his wife, Celiast (Helen), from *History of the Pacific Northwest: Oregon and Washington,* vol. 2, Portland, Oregon: North Pacific History Co., 1889, opposite p. 110. CCHS COLLECTION.

The second daughter of Clatsop leader Coboway, Celiast was born around 1802. Her family lived near Point Adams (Fort Stevens State Park) during the summer, but the rains and winds of winter drove them into a sixty-foot long-house along the Lewis and Clark River. She remembered when John Jacob Astor's Pacific Fur Company representatives arrived in 1811 and built a fort on the peninsula that is now Astoria.

As a young adult, Celiast married a much older French-Canadian baker, Basile Poirier, who was employed at the fort. Shortly after they married in 1825, the Hudson's Bay Company changed its headquarters from Fort George to Fort Vancouver, and most of the employees, including Poirier and Celiast, relocated upriver to Vancouver. After six years of marriage and three children together, the marriage broke apart when it was discovered that Poirier was already married to a woman in Canada.

The same year, 1832, twenty-three-year-old Solomon Smith of New Hampshire was making his way west across the plains with Captain Nathaniel Wyeth's overland expedition. After two Indian attacks, most of the party had deserted and returned to the east, but Smith and six other Americans pressed on and sought refuge with the Canadian and British staff at Fort Vancouver. After learning that Smith had attended a postsecondary academy in Vermont, Dr. John McLoughlin, head of the fort, hired him to teach the half-native children of many fort employees. Smith delivered his instruction in Chinook Jargon and earned $80 per month for two nine-month schoolyears. During his tenure at Fort Vancouver, he met Celiast.

Solomon Smith soon moved to French Prairie to join Celiast, who was living with her sister and brother-in-law, Joseph Gervais. The couple married, purchased a farm, and opened a school in the Gervais home. In 1839, their first son Silas was born, and Celiast convinced Solomon to file for a land claim on Clatsop Plains near her childhood home. In 1840, they settled with their infant son on a land claim between the Skipanon River and the ocean beach, near what is today Smith Lake. One mile south of their home, they helped build a mission and school for the children of settlers and Clatsop Indians. Solomon and Celiast taught local Clatsops as well as their own children.

*In an amazing trek, he herded fifty-five cattle from the Willamette Valley to Tillamook Bay.*

In addition to teaching, Solomon made important contributions to the development of Clatsop County. He introduced wheat, barley, oats, apple trees, cattle, and horses to the area. In an amazing trek with Indian guides and packhorses, he herded fifty-five cattle from the Willamette Valley to Tillamook Bay and over Tillamook Head to his ranch. In 1841, Solomon established the first ferry service across Youngs Bay by lashing two canoes together. He opened a general store on the Skipanon River after supplying provisions for the crews of the shipwrecked *Peacock* (1841) and *Shark* (1846). When the growing number of settlers made it necessary to form a county government in 1843, Smith hosted the meetings at his home until the Clatsop County seat was established on John McClure's land claim in Astoria in 1851. Late in his career, Smith served as state senator for Clatsop and Columbia Counties for two years until his death in 1876. Celiast survived Solomon for a number of years. Her biography in the 1889 *History of the Pacific Northwest: Oregon and Washington* describes her as "a venerable woman."

During their lives in Clatsop County, both Solomon and Celiast developed reputations for public service and generosity. Celiast, described in a *Daily Astorian* article as "warm as summer sunshine," intervened to dispel conflicts between natives and whites on several occasions. Solomon was loved and respected throughout the Northwest, and particularly within his extensive network of family and friends. In a letter to his adult daughter Charlotte and grandson Hank, who lived in Portland in 1875, he demonstrated his desire to share what he had learned during his life: "Tell Hank that his grandfather put in a few apple trees just to let him see what our apples are like."

# Truman Powers

)(

## By Amy Hoffman Couture

In the mid-nineteenth century, many Oregonians believed Astoria was destined to become a metropolis, even a sister city to San Francisco or New York. Like many early pioneers, Truman P. Powers relocated from the Willamette Valley to a donation land claim in Clatsop County, where he believed he would be among the founders of a great city at the mouth of the Columbia.

Powers was born in Vermont in about 1807. Historical records are unclear about how he came to Oregon in the 1840s. According to his adopted daughter Mary, he "crossed the plains" for Oregon in 1846 and met his future wife, a native of Virginia, along the way.

The Powers family arrived in Oregon by 1847 and applied for a donation land claim in Yamhill County. Truman taught school near Oregon City for about a year, but he wanted to settle at the mouth of the Columbia. In 1848 he abandoned his Yamhill claim and took a claim at Baker's Bay, near present-day Chinook, Washington. Two months later, in June 1848, the Powers family settled on a land claim on the west side of the Lewis and Clark River near Astoria.

As an active member of the newly formed Clatsop Plains Pioneer Presbyterian Church, Powers developed friendships with pioneer members

Drawing of Truman P. Powers from *History of the Pacific Northwest:
Oregon and Washington,* vol. 2, Portland, Oregon: North Pacific History Co.,
1889, opposite p. 42. CCHS COLLECTION.

of the church community such as John Adair, R. W. Morrison, and William
H. Gray, and taught Sunday school to their children. In 1937, Powers posthu-
mously became one of the first two elected elders of the church.

Powers was also active in territorial and state government. In 1850, he was a
member of the Oregon territorial legislature, representing Clatsop County.

In 1852, he became treasurer of a short-lived mint operation. As the
California Gold Rush was winding down, merchants and former gold seek-
ers returned to Oregon with at least two million dollars' worth of gold dust.
Oregonians decided to mint their own currency with two types of solid gold
coins. The operation violated federal law, and Oregon's Governor Lane quickly
shut it down.

In about 1856, the Powers family left their farm on the Lewis and Clark
River and moved to a home in Astoria. Powers taught in a one-room school-
house in Upper Astoria then helped to build one of the city's first schools.
During his career, he also served as a postmaster, customs collector, and school
clerk. In 1975, he was president of the Oregon Pioneer and Historical Society.
The organization, founded by William H. Gray in 1872, eventually grew into
today's Clatsop County Historical Society.

Powers lived in the city until he died in 1883. In his will, he left eighty acres in Upper Astoria jointly to his son-in-law, Christian Linenweber, and to a representative of the Presbyterian Church, William Wadhams, setting off a complicated legal battle that ended when the court sided with Powers' son-in-law. In a short biography of her father, written after his death, his daughter Mary recalled that he "never lost faith in Astoria becoming a large city."

# William H. Gray

)(

## By Amy Hoffman Couture

As a young man, William H. Gray was so arrogant and difficult to get along with that his own minister said he had "confidence in his own abilities to a fault" and he "by no means [had] the qualifications [as a minister] that we think desirable." Yet by the end of his life, Gray was identified with so many aspects of the state's early development that he was respected throughout the Northwest.

William H. Gray had nine older siblings when he was born in upstate New York in 1810. An orphan by age fourteen, he apprenticed with a carpenter until

View of Waiilatpu before 1847, from *Historic Sketches: Walla Walla, Whitman, Columbia and Garfield Counties, Washington Territory*, by Frank T. Gilbert, Portland, Oregon: A. G. Walling, 1882. CCHS Collection.

he was twenty-one. In 1836 Gray was living with a local Presbyterian minister when a letter arrived from Dr. Marcus Whitman, who was looking for an assistant to help him build a mission in Walla Walla, Washington.

Gray was hired as a secular carpenter and accompanied Whitman, his wife Narcissa, and their party to Oregon Territory. Upon their arrival in September 1836, Gray constructed the first buildings at missions near Walla Walla and Lewiston, Idaho.

The following spring, Gray expressed interest in building his own mission in western Montana, but he needed provisions. Intending to trade horses for cattle in Missouri, he proceeded east with twenty horses, several Canadians, and five Indian guides. At the Green River Fur Rendezvous, he ignored Jim Bridger's warnings of hostile Sioux raiding parties to the east. Two weeks later, a large group of Sioux attacked, stole his horses, and killed all the Indians in his party. Years later, Gray told his son he had saved himself by playing hymns on a small flute. When the Flathead Indians near his intended mission site learned about the attack, they apparently believed he had sacrificed the Indians for his own survival and that of his white companions. Believing his reputation in the area was ruined, he gave up plans to build a mission there.

*Two weeks later, a large group of Sioux attacked, stole his horses, and killed all the Indians in his party.*

Gray returned to New York, attended classes at a medical school for several months, and married Mary Augusta Dix after a two-week courtship. With his wife, he returned to the west in the spring of 1838 in a party that included John Sutter, the founder of Sutter's Fort in Sacramento, California. Again working as a carpenter at the Whitman Mission later in 1838, Gray sought to build his own mission under the direction of Henry Spalding, Whitman's partner. Spalding did not approve of Gray's intended location, however, so Gray abruptly resigned and left the Whitman Mission in 1842.

Again using his carpentry skills, he took a job building the campus of what would later become Willamette University, but was at the time a small school for educating missionaries' children. Wagon trains of settlers were arriving in the Willamette Valley, and Gray recognized the need for a regional government.

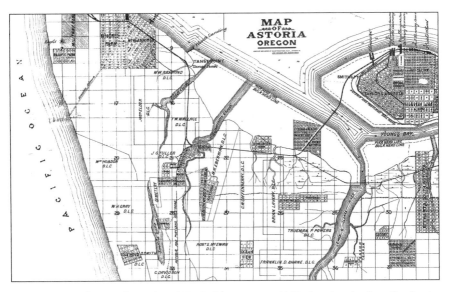

Left portion of a map drawn by W. H. Cuthbertson, ca. 1899, showing the donation land claims of Solomon H. Smith, Truman Powers, and William H. Gray. CCHS COLLECTION.

He served on an early planning committee and then as secretary at a meeting in Champoeg, Oregon, in May 1843, when Oregonians voted to form a provisional government with ties to the United States, rather than to Great Britain. He helped to write the provisional government's constitution, to form Oregon's first militia, and to initiate a law providing free public education for Oregon's children.

In 1846, Gray, his wife, and their five young children settled on a land claim in Clatsop County between the ocean beach and what is today Oceanview Cemetery in Warrenton. Gray continued to involve himself in community planning. From his home, he organized the Clatsop Plains Pioneer Presbyterian Church and ran a

William H. Gray, ca. 1850.

COURTESY OF THE CLATSOP PRESBYTERIAN

CHURCH. CCHS COLLECTION.

79

LEFT: Portrait of William H. Gray, ca. 1880. CCHS 1501.A. RIGHT: Portrait of Mrs. Mary Augusta Dix Gray, wife of William H. Gray, ca. 1880. CCHS 11501.B.13.

boarding school. In the early 1850s, he was a member of the school board and served as county commissioner.

After attempting to make a living on his farm for about a decade, Gray and his growing family left Clatsop County in 1858. He tried mining in the Cascades, then he built a boat for transporting cargo on the Upper Columbia River.

By 1867, when the United States Secretary of State, William Seward, traveled to Alaska to purchase the territory from Russia, he chose Gray to accompany him because of Gray's extensive knowledge of Pacific Northwest Indians' languages and customs, a tribute to Gray's growing reputation.

From Alaska, Gray returned to Astoria, where he wrote a lengthy book which he published in Portland in 1870 under the title *A History of Oregon, 1792–1849, Drawn from Personal Observation and Authentic Information*. Although the book was generally well received, his descriptions of the poor treatment of Indians by missionaries and white settlers provoked controversy. The *Weekly Astorian* reported in 1877 that when a critic questioned the portrayal of the missionaries in his book, Gray dismissed the criticisms as "the foolish ravings of a fanatic." During the same period, he worked to secure funds to erect a monument honoring Marcus and Narcissa Whitman at Waiilatpu.

After his daughter Caroline married Jacob Kamm, a businessman with land in Olney, Gray and his wife retired to Olney and managed the farm. His wife died in 1881. Gray died eight years later and was buried at Hillside Pioneer Cemetery in Astoria. He and his wife were reinterred in 1916 at the historic Whitman Mission site, which Gray had worked to establish.

When William H. Gray died in 1889, he left four sons and three daughters. The *Daily Morning Astorian* published a highly complimentary article about his life. "No man knew more of Oregon," the newspaper proclaimed. "He was an encyclopedia of pioneer information."

# Cyrus Olney

## By Nancy Hoffman

Owning property was more lucrative than being a frontier judge, as Cyrus Olney proved.

Olney was born in 1815 in New York. His father moved the family several times, from New York to Pennsylvania to Iowa, instilling a westward drive in his children. Olney was drawn to the law as a young man. After a year at Marietta College in 1837–1838, he served a legal apprenticeship and was admitted to the Iowa bar. He worked as an attorney until Iowa became a state in 1846, then he was elected to a four-year judgeship paying $1,000 a year.

In the meantime, his brother Nathan had moved further west to The Dalles, Oregon, where he worked as a trader,

Judge Cyrus Olney, ca. 1865.

soldier, Indian agent, and fur trapper. In 1851, Cyrus resigned his Iowa judgeship and, with his wife Sarah, left to join Nathan. He was admitted to the bar of the Oregon Territory in December. A little over a year later, President Pierce appointed him Associate Justice of the Supreme Court of Oregon Territory and assigned him to a northwest Oregon district that included Portland and Clatsop County. While traveling through his assigned territory, he joined one of the first parties to scale Mount Hood. He also served in the First Regiment of Oregon Volunteers, an army unit mustered to protect settlers from Indian attack.

*Cyrus's brother Nathan was gravely injured in a skirmish with hostile Indians when his skull was penetrated by an arrowhead that could not be removed.*

Cyrus's brother Nathan was gravely injured in a skirmish with hostile Indians when his skull was penetrated by an arrowhead that could not be removed. Cyrus was making very little money, so he resigned his Oregon judgeship in 1857 and joined his brother in the fur trade. They made one trip across the Pacific with a shipment of furs. But upon their return, Nathan fell from a horse, causing the arrowhead previously lodged in his skull to penetrate his brain and kill him.

Olney then moved his family to Astoria, where he made his first solid investment: he purchased the John McClure claim to the western half of the city. He then platted some of his claim into lots and raffled the lots in the "Olney Lottery." Each person who purchased a lot for $50 had an opportunity to win the grand prize, a house and two lots on Twelfth Street between Franklin and Exchange.

In 1863, Olney became the superintendent of Astoria's schools with a salary not to exceed $50 a year. Several of his brothers and sisters joined him in Astoria, but his own family failed to thrive. Four of his children died in infancy, and his wife died in January 1864, leaving three children, eleven, eight, and one. All three died before their father did.

In 1866, Cyrus Olney was elected to the State Senate, and in 1870, he began a term in Oregon's House of Representatives. He became ill shortly after arriving in Salem and died in Astoria on December 23, 1870. He was buried in the Old Cemetery at the top of the hill in Astoria.

Cyrus Olney, ca. 1865. Oregon Historical Society, OrHi 3540.

Before he died, Olney wrote out a will by hand, naming two executors and bequeathing his entire estate to the city of Astoria. Almost immediately his siblings came forward to contest the will. They pointed out that he had been under the effect of opiates to treat his illness and therefore was not in his right mind. The case languished in the courts for years. A small article in a November 1879 *Daily Astorian* noted that the family was more concerned about getting his money than about maintaining his neglected gravesite. In 1877, the estate was determined to be worth over $100,000 (close to two million dollars today), and the court found in favor of the family in 1879, declaring that Olney had been insane.

After his death, Cyrus Olney was recognized in two ways. Olney School was built near the corner of Klaskanine and Fourth Streets in Astoria, and a post office with his name in what is now the town of Olney was established in 1875.

# Jennie Michel

By Amy Hoffman Couture

In 1829, the Chief Factor of the Hudson's Bay Company at Fort Vancouver, John McLoughlin, ordered a deadly assault on the Clatsop village at Tansy Point, near present-day Warrenton. A British bark, the *William and Anne*, had gone aground near the village two months earlier, and the Clatsop Indians

Jennie Michel with one of her baskets, ca. 1900. CCHS 3682.005.

LEFT: Jennie Michel at the site of the Lewis and Clark salt cairn in Seaside, Oregon, ca. 1903. CCHS 11191.005. RIGHT: Jennie Michel, photographed by George M. Weister. From *A Short History of Oregon* by Sidona Viola Johnson, published in Chicago by A. C. McClurg and Co., 1904. CCHS COLLECTION.

refused to relinquish the cargo from the wrecked vessel. Furious at the Clatsops' defiance and suspecting they had murdered the ship's crew, McLoughlin sent a troop of a hundred men to attack the village if the Clatsops continued to resist. The Indians remained defiant, and McLoughlin's men fired on the village. Jennie Michel, whose family lived in the village, was thirteen at the time. Even as an old woman, she vividly recalled the trauma of the attack.

Jennie Michel's Clatsop name was Tsin-is-tum. She was born around 1816. Ten years earlier, Lewis and Clark had wintered at Fort Clatsop. The Indians at first feared the expedition had arrived "to make war on them," as Michel recalled in a 1900 interview with a historian from the Oregon Historical Society. Soon relations were friendly between Lewis and Clark and the Clatsops, and Tsin-is-tum's uncle, Ka-ta-ta, hunted elk with the expedition's hunters. Lewis and Clark estimated that two hundred Clatsops lived in the area in 1806.

In 1811, about five years before Tsin-is-tum was born, employees of the Pacific Fur Company established Fort Astoria on the site of present-day Astoria.

Throughout the 1810s and 1820s, her village participated in the fur trade and had frequent friendly contact with staff at the fort and with trading vessels from Britain and the United States.

In 1829, when the attack on her village began, Tsin-is-tum ran frantically with her mother into the forest to escape the shelling. As they ran, her mother carried Tsin-is-tum's younger sister on her shoulders. A tree branch cut the girl's eye, leaving her blind in that eye for the rest of her life. Tsin-is-tum recalled that her sister was thereafter known as "Squint Eye." Along with several other Clatsop leaders, Tsin-is-tum's father died in the attack on the village.

Twelve years later, an American who visited Point Adams found the Clatsops still living in their traditional plank houses and eating fish, venison, and berries, but a defensive wall now stood around the village. He estimated that 160 Clatsops remained.

During this period, Tsin-is-tum married the Nehalem chief Wah-tat-kum. They lived "along the coast between the Columbia and Nehalem Rivers many years until he died," as Michel recounted. Her second husband was Michel Martineau, a former resident of Clark County and an employee of John McLoughlin's, who was some eight years her junior. Martineau died in 1902; his wife survived him by three years.

*❧ Dart promised to allow the Clatsops to remain at Point Adams, but the U.S. Senate refused to recognize the treaty. ❧*

The year 1851 was significant for all the native people in the north coast area. It was the year the Oregon Superintendent of Indian Affairs, Anson Dart, met with local tribes at Tansy Point to negotiate treaties. The Clatsops expressed their frustration over frequent steamships in their fishing areas and two noisy sawmills near their village. They were also angry that the Donation Land Law of 1850 had allowed settlers to procure free land within Clatsop territory then sell it for a profit. Farms, livestock ranches, and dairies now covered their former hunting grounds on Clatsop Plains. Dart promised to allow the Clatsops to remain at Point Adams in exchange for approximately 500,000 acres on Clatsop Plains, but the U.S. Senate refused to recognize the treaty. The Clatsops would not receive federal protection, recognition, or

Jennie Michel, said to be 101 years old, making a mat of rushes. CCHS 4299.005B.

specific land for a reservation. Dart noted that the Clatsops now numbered a mere eighty.

Between 1851 and 1900, most of the remaining Clatsops died of diseases introduced by settlers and traders. At the turn of the century, Tsin-is-tum, now known as Jennie Michel, was a well-known figure in Oregon because she was one of the last full-blooded Clatsops still living. She knew how to weave grass baskets, spoke a Chinook language, and remembered old stories about the area's history. She described her mother's memory of Lewis and Clark's salt-works operation in present-day Seaside, where members of the expedition boiled sea water to produce salt for their return journey to Missouri. As Michel recalled, "All the Indians came and camped near the salt makers." Her testimony about the location of the site and the formation of the rocks, "built up all around as high as the head of a small child," helped to establish the salt works as a historic site.

Locals, tourists, and historians trained their cameras on Jennie Michel so often that her 1905 obituary suggested she had been photographed more than any other Oregonian. In most of the surviving images, she is pictured alone, with long, dry grasses she is weaving into a basket.

# Adam Van Dusen

## By M. J. Cody

There were only two frame houses in Astoria when Caroline and Adam Van Dusen settled there in the spring of 1849. The young couple were resilient—Caroline noted that they had very much enjoyed the previous year's Oregon Trail wagon trek from Michigan. But the miserable, frozen winter at their Youngs Bay land claim proved too much. They opted for a more civilized location in Astoria proper. The energetic, well-liked couple adapted quickly to their new home. They fixed up the "Shark" house, a poorly constructed log cabin built by sailors from the *Shark* shipwreck of 1846, and Adam soon was involved in Provisional Government matters. Van Dusen served as one of the judges of election for the precinct of Astoria and as juror in legal cases, including indictments for selling "spirituous liquor" to Indians. In one such case against John W. Champ, a repeat offender in illegally dispensing liquor, Van Dusen not only sat as juror, but held Champ's $1,000 security, similar to a bail bond.

In the 1850 census, at age twenty-seven, Van Dusen was listed as "hotel keeper" with $2,000 in assets, although it is unknown what hotel that may have been. He soon built a frame house and established the A. Van Dusen Co. store, where he was the first merchant in Astoria to sell goods from shelves (Hudson's Bay Company sold their stock from boxes). An 1877 *Weekly Astorian* item noted that "the firm has sold as high as $1,200 a day, when times were flush here."

Adam Van Dusen, ca. 1880.

CCHS 14951.00V.

Adam Van Dusen, ca. 1860. CCHS 14956.00V.

The first flush times in Astoria were during the 1848–1864 California Gold Rush, when the port vigorously exported supplies. Union Army Generals Ulysses S. Grant, Philip Sheridan, Joseph Hooker, and other military dignitaries visited Van Dusen's store and drank "toddies" in the back room. One account refers to Van Dusen abiding the convivial consumption of alcohol while humming a well-known tune, "cold water give to me, for I am a teetotaler, from drinking customs, free."

As a member of the Board of Trustees of the Town of Astoria from 1856 to the 1870s, Van Dusen was involved in city ordinances and finance, platting, and building infrastructure. He was a prominent Freemason and an agent with Hiram Brown for Wells Fargo financial services.

Adam Van Dusen with his family, ca. 1857. From left to right: Cara, wife Caroline, Florence, Adam, and Brenham Van Dusen. Three more children—Hustler, Lloyd, and Mary Amy—would follow. CCHS 14953.00V.

The Van Dusens had six children, three girls and three boys. In 1863, they moved to a large new home at Sixteenth and Franklin (currently the location of the old Columbia Hospital), where they entertained friends and prominent visitors to the city. The couple loved to dance, as reported in an 1875 letter to the newspaper's editor: "Many is the time I have tripped the light fantastic with A. Van Dusen and his sparkling wife Caroline," wrote A. B. McKean.

*Weekly Astorian* newspaper articles in 1878 relate many Van Dusen doings. Adam was on the Firemen's Grand Dress Ball Honorary Committee, daughter Florence taught music, daughter Cara opened a private school, and a choir benefit at the Van Dusens' church, Grace Episcopal, was "one of the most social and enjoyable gatherings ever met together in Astoria." There were intimate family items on the Van Dusen children, including the report that "our young friend Lloyd Van Dusen is laid up with a hand, sorely cut with a knife."

Sons Lloyd, Brenham, and Hustler were clerks in their father's store before taking over the business. In 1879, an advertisement in the *Weekly Astorian* announced, "If you are in want of a suit or a suit of clothes of the latest style and pattern go to A. Van Dusen & Co. and Brenham will fit you a-la-mode." Hustler and Brenham later branched out into real estate and insurance.

Adam Van Dusen, age sixty-one, died June 24, 1884. Caroline continued to live in their stately home, entertaining friends and family until her death in 1910 at age eighty-five.

Many descendants of the Van Dusens still live in the area, including Astoria's longtime mayor Willis Van Dusen, elected in 1991 and still in office in 2009.

# J. G. Hustler

## By Amy Hoffman Couture

Captain Jackson Gregory Hustler was one of the first Columbia River bar pilots in 1850s Astoria. As a mid-nineteenth-century seafarer, he witnessed the slave trade in the North Atlantic, the rush of gold-seekers to California, and the loss of ships in the dangerous waters at the entrance to the Columbia River.

Hustler was born in New York City in 1826 and began his long career at sea at age thirteen. At eighteen, he joined the U.S. Navy and was one of 132 sailors on a ship in a squadron that patrolled West African waters to intercept slave-trading vessels. The well-known U.S.S. *Constitution,* "Old Ironsides," was in the same squadron. An epidemic of yellow fever decimated the crew of Hustler's ship in 1844, but he and thirteen others survived and managed to sail to head-quarters in the Cape Verde Islands.

Back in New York, Hustler worked as a harbor pilot for the next five years. When the California Gold Rush began in 1849, he sailed to San Francisco. After a few months in the Sierra Nevada gold country, he decided to resume his

Portrait of J. G. Hustler, ca. 1875.

CCHS 1574.00H.

J. G. Hustler, ca. 1880. CCHS 4470.00H.

Early pilots on the Columbia River bar. From left to right, Captains Asa Cole Farnsworth,
J. G. Hustler, Charles Edwards, Moses Rogers, and Alfred Crosby, ca. 1853. CCHS 4853.375.

The *Eliza Anderson,* a paddlewheeler piloted by J. G. Hustler, ca. 1900. CCHS 541.340.

piloting career. Hustler and a partner, Captain Cornelius White, purchased the schooner *Mary Taylor* in San Francisco. The *Mary Taylor* had been a pilot boat in New York before sailing to Alaska and California and was probably very similar to the boat Hustler had piloted in New York harbor. Hustler and White sailed the schooner up the Pacific coast to Astoria, arriving on Christmas Day, 1849.

With J. G. Hustler at the helm, the *Mary Taylor* became the first vessel to regularly pilot ships across the treacherous Columbia River bar. In 1852, when a board of pilot commissioners was established in Astoria, Hustler officially received his bar pilot license. Captain George Flavel then hired Hustler to pilot the 140-foot steamship *Eliza Anderson* and the barkentine *Jane A. Falkenberg.*

> ℮ *Captain George Flavel then hired Hustler to pilot the 140-foot steamship* Eliza Anderson *and the barkentine* Jane A. Falkenberg. ℮

In 1852, Hustler married a local woman, Eliza McKean, who had settled in Astoria in 1848 after she crossed the plains with her family and narrowly missed the Whitman Mission massacre. Hustler and his wife had at least two children,

The barkentine *Jane A. Falkenberg,* piloted by J. G. Hustler.
Painting by Cleveland Rockwell, 1884. FLAVEL COLLECTION, CCHS 465.001.

Mary and Maggy, and the family settled in a new, bright-white house on Duane Avenue between Ninth and Tenth Streets. The Hustlers' residence was unusually ornate and expensive for early Astoria. In the 1870s, when other walkways in Astoria were muddy or wooden, the Hustlers were the first people in town to pave an "artificial stone" sidewalk in front of their home.

John T. Halloran, editor of the newspaper the *Astorian* in the 1880s, wrote one of the few contemporary accounts of Hustler's personality. Notoriously harsh in his vivid descriptions of local people, Halloran described Hustler as a "big blustering fellow" who was known to "vomit forth an issue of unclean words" when under the influence of alcohol. Hustler's niece, Polly McKean Bell, gave a very different account. She fondly remembered her uncle as a shy man who brought gifts to her family on New Year's Day and "knew how to compliment the ladies, young and old."

In addition to his career as a harbor and bar pilot, Hustler purchased real estate in Astoria and worked as city treasurer and school district clerk. In 1893, he died of pneumonia at age sixty-seven. His wife Eliza lived until 1935, becoming the community's oldest living pioneer.

# P. W. Gillette

## By Liisa Penner

In 1852, Preston W. Gillette left his home in Ohio intending to pioneer the horticultural business somewhere in the lands along the Pacific. Shortly after setting off on his great adventure, he became ill with smallpox and had to interrupt his journey. A few weeks later, still weak, he gathered his gear together and again set out across the plains.

After much searching, he found a piece of property along the east side of the Lewis and Clark River in Clatsop County, Oregon, and began to till the land. First he put in a vegetable garden. The next year his father sent bundles of trees, shrubs, bulbs, and roots,

Preston W. Gillette, ca. 1875.

which he planted with care. A few years later, in early 1861, he wrote in a journal he kept faithfully through the years: "My cattle, horses and sheep are growing and increasing around me. My orchards are enlarging, bearing and promising abundance; and my bees are gathering honey for me from every flower." When it was too stormy to work outside, Gillette spent quiet hours by the wood stove, reading books and newspapers and writing political letters.

This was his design for life: hard work promising ever greater returns, along with plenty of time for study and reflection and appreciating nature. "I have vainly sought for words with which to describe this most beautiful spring day, but language is inadequate. It cannot

Drawing, unknown provenance, ca. 1905.

CCHS Collection.

95

Preston W. Gillette with son (at far right) at the site of the former Fort Clatsop, which he and other pioneers helped to identify. At left is Silas Smith, and near center, with long coat, is Carlos W. Shane. Photographed June 9, 1900. CCHS 11190.796.

be described. It can only be seen and felt," he wrote in his journal on April 15, 1861.

Gillette was alarmed to read in the newspapers that the growing aggression between the North and the South had led to the start of a bloody civil war. "What have we done to incite this rebellion?" he wrote in his journal on May 12, 1861. "Nothing. We have Right, Justice, and the Law on our side, and the South have been the aggressor. These are facts. I say that if war is the word, let it come."

June rains came, and still he worked. "It has been raining and misting nearly all day and yet I plowed potatoes nearly all day," he wrote. The loneliness of his home in the woods became intolerable. His nearest neighbors, the family of Joseph Jeffers, were two miles downriver, a strenuous pull on the oars in his small rowboat. If he wanted to go to town, he had to make the long trip to the Jeffers' place, continue a bit further north, then row across Youngs Bay to Astoria. Sometimes he made the return trips in the rain, working against tide and wind. In an effort to dispel the loneliness, Gillette

> *The loneliness of his home in the woods became intolerable.*

and his neighbor Jeffers' son Elijah began clearing a trail through the woods between the two houses. The day the paths met was a time for celebration.

On June 13, 1861, Gillette wrote in his journal: "I have had an ill temper today—everything seems to have went wrong—I went out and milked in the rain and mud amid myriads of savage gnats and on my way to the house, I slipped and fell into the mud and spilt the bucket of milk all over me. Getting ever so angry did not repair the damages. I worked in the mud for two or three hours on the moor fixing bridges and I plowed potatoes about two hours and set out a lot of cabbage plants. The storm is now raging with the violence of a winter storm."

The next day he discovered that some animal had killed half a dozen of his chickens. Each day he had to hunt down his horse and cows that had wandered into the woods in search of something to eat. Some of his calves died of starvation. Even his cat disappeared.

*❧ I milked in the rain and mud amid myriads of savage gnats and on my way to the house, I slipped and fell into the mud and spilt the bucket of milk all over me. ❧*

Divisions in the local community sharpened as the war continued. Gillette felt compelled to persuade others of his views. He took on temporary government work, assessing taxes and serving as customs inspector, among other duties, neglecting his farm on the Lewis and Clark River. A few years later, he was elected to the Oregon State Legislature. The farm had lost its appeal, and he sold it in 1867. Moving to Portland, he became successful in the real-estate business.

Today a paved road connects the Gillette farm with the Jeffers farm and with Astoria beyond. The whole trip now takes no more than fifteen minutes by car. The fields Gillette worked so hard to clear can still be seen, but his fruit orchards and vegetable gardens belong to the past.

# Bridget Grant

## By Nancy Hoffman

When she died in 1923 at age ninety-two, no official mention was made of Bridget Grant's storied past. Having raised a family of three daughters and five sons, she had become a respected resident of Astoria. But Grant was much more than a mother and solid citizen. She was a prime player in some of Astoria's seedier history.

Bridget emigrated from Ireland and met and married Peter Grant in Gloucester, Massachusetts, in 1845. After operating boarding houses in Gloucester and San Francisco, the couple arrived in Astoria in 1876. Peter drowned soon after their arrival, and Bridget was forced to manage their boarding house on Commercial Street between Fourteenth and Fifteenth on her own.

Photo portrait of Bridget Grant, ca. 1905. CCHS 5597.00G.

Bridget Grant, front center, with her sons and daughters, ca. 1910. Her
daughters were Kate Lighter, Margaret Barry, and Mary Ellen Lemon. Sons were
Peter, John F. (Jack), Alex, William, and Ignatius (Nace). CCHS 8665.00G.

Astoria was a bustling seaport in the late nineteenth century. Sailing ships
arrived from around the world, bringing immigrant labor to the canneries,
transporting logs to sawmills down the Pacific
coast, or exporting salmon. And sailing ships
needed men—unskilled sailors quickly learned to
furl and unfurl the huge canvas sails and keep the
ships moving. Large crews were hard to come by,
since better, more lucrative work was plentiful. So
a new enterprise developed, known originally as
"crimping" and later as "shanghaiing" (a reference
to the destination of many of the ships).

*❧ Bridget's role as a crimp is not well documented . . . but she was legendary in Portland for shanghaiing and extortion. ☙*

Ship captains who needed to fill out a crew
would contract with crimps, usually for the victims'
first two months' pay. The crimps used a variety of
tactics, most often involving alcohol, to trick unwitting young men—farmers,
loggers, sailors, anyone who fit the bill—onto the boats.

Bridget's role as a crimp is not well documented, perhaps because crimping
was illegal and she covered her tracks. But she was legendary in Portland for

shanghaiing and extortion. Her sons Peter and Jack managed a boarding house that she owned in Portland, and Peter was indicted for shanghaiing activities in partnership with a renowned Portland crimp, John Sullivan.

Astoria in 1867. CCHS 194.900.

Astoria seaport, with steamship, log raft, fishing boats, and small tugs, late nineteenth centu

Bridget's most infamous exploits involved her farm in the Walluski area along the Youngs River south of Astoria. She is reported to have lured men there with the promise of work clearing the land. In fact, she used the farm as a place to gather crews for ship captains. The kidnapped men would be gathered up at gun point or invited to a drinking party. In either case, they would soon find themselves on a ship miles away from home, where they would be forced to work for nothing.

By the turn of the century, shanghaiing had mostly disappeared. New laws made it a federal crime, and steamships requiring smaller, more skilled crews were rapidly replacing sailing ships. Bridget retired to her farm in 1905 at the age of seventy-four.

Her family contributed to her rise in respectability in Astoria. All three daughters became schoolteachers, and one married the chief of police. A son became co-owner of an oyster farm, and another became the Walluski Grange Master. Although members of her family owned and operated the Astoria Wine Company as well as a saloon on Commercial Street, the North Pacific Brewing Company, Bridget outlived her seamy reputation.

the background are canneries built up on piers. Columbia River Maritime Museum 1984.49.2.tif.

# Cleveland Rockwell

)(

## By Nancy Hoffman

Cleveland Rockwell is a well-known landscape artist and engineer of the late nineteenth century. For many years he surveyed and mapped Astoria and the surrounding area as well as capturing the beauty at the mouth of the Columbia through his art. Although he never maintained a formal residence in Astoria, he spent months camped along the shore. Some of his more famous paintings of the area include *Early Morning View of Tongue Point from Astoria, Salmon Fishing Grounds—Mouth of the Columbia, Crossing the Bar,* and *Looking Toward Saddle Mountain from Baker Bay.* He was also responsible for the survey work that led to building a railroad trestle across Youngs Bay.

Rockwell was born November 24, 1837, in Youngstown, Ohio. When he was eighteen, he joined the U.S. Coast Survey as an aide. The mission of the Coast Survey was to provide accurate maps of both coasts, and Rockwell spent the next thirty-six years surveying, mapping, and sketching the rivers and coastlines of both the Atlantic and the Pacific.

Rockwell's first assignment involved a section of New York harbor. His excellent work led to a 1958 assignment that took him to Charleston harbor and along the coast of South Carolina. He was also attending school. Between his education and his experience, he became knowledgeable in astronomy, topography, and hydrology.

When the Civil War broke out, Rockwell was quickly put to work charting the

Cleveland Rockwell, ca. 1870. Courtesy of the Columbia River Maritime Museum.

Cleveland Rockwell, ca. 1875. OREGON HISTORICAL SOCIETY, OrHi 25125.

Atlantic islands and coastline. (It was important militarily to know where Southern ships might hide.) In 1863 he joined the Union Army as Captain of Engineers, Topographical Corps, Army of the Ohio. He continued to serve to the end of the war and participated in Sherman's devastating march to the sea. After the war, he joined a group of scientists traveling to South America to chart the rivers and coasts of Colombia. Upon his return, the Coast Survey rehired him and sent him to San Francisco. He spent the rest of his career on the West Coast.

Rockwell's occupation was affected by the seasons. He spent spring and summer gathering data by hiking and boating into remote, uncharted areas and using triangulation to accurately set locations. In fall and winter, he charted the

*The Columbia River Bar,* oil painting by Cleveland Rockwell, 1884. CCHS 282.

information he had found. He began with pencil, finalized with ink, then produced copper plate engravings. The charts were ultimately sent to Washington, D.C.

Rockwell arrived in San Francisco in 1867. By July 1868, he was organizing a survey party out of Astoria. Over the next twenty-five years, he surveyed and charted the mouth of the John Day River, Cape Disappointment, Youngs Bay, Baker Bay, Point Adams, Cathlamet Bay, Tongue Point, and the Columbia River all the way to Portland. Until his transfer to Portland in 1878, he worked around the Columbia each summer and spent the rest of the year in California.

In 1873, he married fourteen-year-old Cornelia Flemming Russell. Rockwell was thirty-six, and Cornelia's parents adamantly opposed the marriage. The age difference and their daughter's youth were not their only concerns. The Russell family was from Tennessee, and they condemned Rockwell's service in the Union Army, particularly his connection with Sherman's Raiders. Despite her parents' protests, Cornelia married Rockwell on a ferryboat in San Francisco Bay. In the course of their marriage, Cleveland and Cornelia had several children who died in infancy from either measles or scarlet fever. Two girls lived to maturity and were important in Rockwell's life. Gertrude Ellinor Rockwell was born July 10, 1881, followed by Cornelia (Neely) Rockwell the next year.

During his lifetime, Rockwell received significant recognition for the detail and accuracy of his work. As he traveled, he sketched the geography he found, often including sketches in his reports to the Coast Survey. He also painted watercolors and oils, giving them to friends and family as presents.

Most of Rockwell's life is fully documented because of his employment with the Coast Survey. Where he was stationed at any given time, which part of the Columbia he might be surveying, even the days he took for vacation are public record. But there is a long-standing mystery. Shortly after his father died in February 1874, Rockwell took a year's leave of absence. The first four months were paid leave, and he spent them finishing up some survey charts. After that, historians can only speculate. Some believe he spent eight months in Ohio clearing up his father's affairs. The fact that he retired a

*⊚ During his lifetime, Rockwell received significant recognition for the detail and accuracy of his work. ⊚*

rich man from the Coast Survey, which paid poorly, suggests that he inherited a sizable fortune. Others believe he spent the eight months in Europe receiving more art instruction. His skill as an artist lends support to this claim.

An 1889 controversy in Astoria testifies to Rockwell's pride in his work. The Astoria Chamber of Commerce requested a resurvey of the river front to

*Captain Flavel's Tug,* oil painting by Cleveland Rockwell, 1884. Captain Flavel's tugboat leads a ship across the dangerous Columbia River bar. CCHS 152.

account for wharves, canneries, and landings not included in the original survey. They also asked for a survey of Youngs Bay for the possible construction of a railroad trestle. Although Rockwell disagreed with the need to resurvey the river front (because the river pilots had not asked for it) and doubted the viability of the location chosen for the trestle, he surveyed the area carefully and completely. Then he filed his report with the Coast Survey.

*⌖ Rockwell said that he did not have time to "make the plot of soundings," but the final report read that he did not have time to "make the soundings." ☙*

A typist transcribing his report inadvertently dropped two words. Rockwell said that he did not have time to "make the plot of soundings," but the final report read that he did not have time to "make the soundings." The difference was critical, and when the editor of the *Daily Astorian,* J. T. Halloran, received a copy of the report, he roasted Rockwell in his newspaper. Rockwell spent the next two years getting the typist to acknowledge her mistake, complaining to the editor of the *Daily Astorian,* and firing off angry notes to the supervisor in San Francisco for releasing a faulty transcript. Finally, after a face-to-face meeting in Washington, D.C., to settle the dispute, Rockwell resigned from the Coast Survey. He was fifty-five years old, Cornelia was thirty-three, Gertrude was twelve, and Neely was ten.

Finally Rockwell could devote his full attention to art. He traveled north to Canada and Alaska with his family. Today museums throughout the country display the sketches and paintings that resulted. Fishing and hiking became passions that inspired numerous sketches of Saddle Mountain. Rockwell also painted on commission and maintained a supply of small watercolors, which he sold to visitors to his home. Several magazines published his fiction and nonfiction stories, and he taught classes in drawing and painting.

Rockwell continued to paint prolifically until the day he died. He finished a small watercolor of the Oregon coast in early 1907 and died of pneumonia on March 22 of that year.

# Charlotte Smith

)(

## By Amy Hoffman Couture

The last full-blooded Clatsop Indians died by the 1920s, and the Clatsop Tribe ceased to exist as a separate cultural group much earlier. But the mixed-race descendants of the original Clatsops often encountered the same racism and social inequality their ancestors experienced, despite their apparent inclusion in Astoria's white community. The life of Charlotte Smith illustrates the troubles that Clatsop descendants, especially women, faced as they attempted to assert their rights and equality in nineteenth-century Astoria.

Charlotte Smith, ca. 1885. Courtesy of Virginia Holdener.

Charlotte Smith and her granddaughter, 1909. Courtesy of Richard Basch.

In October 1840, Charlotte was born in a log cabin on her family's donation land claim near the Skipanon River. She was the fourth of her parents' seven children, who were designated "half-Indian" in the 1850 Clatsop County Census. Her mother, Celiast, was the daughter of the prominent Clatsop leader Coboway. Her father, Solomon, was an early Oregon pioneer from New Hampshire who worked as a teacher for the Hudson's Bay Company in Vancouver as early as 1832, before settling on the Clatsop Plains so his wife could be closer to her family. Solomon and Celiast Smith are known as agricultural pioneers in Clatsop County.

The Smith family was respected for creating a school for the white settlers' children and for their help with negotiations between the Clatsops and the white community. As children, Charlotte and her siblings once helped their mother hide a white settler in their basement in order to protect him from an Indian attack. Her older brother Silas later attended school on the East Coast and became a prominent lawyer in Astoria. But Charlotte struggled to create a safe and stable life for herself. At age twenty-five, she divorced her first husband, Sylvester Ingalls, after about seven years of mar-riage. In the Clatsop County Circuit Court in 1871, Charlotte claimed that among other abuses, Ingalls violated his "marital obligations" by com-mitting "frequent acts of adultery . . . with a certain young woman named 'Jessie.'" Ingalls owned two city lots in Astoria and fifteen acres in the coun-try, and Charlotte worried that he would sell the property before the divorce was finalized, leaving Charlotte and her son destitute.

*In the nineteenth century, legal protections for native women were almost nonexistent.*

Charlotte's second marriage in 1874 to Charles Dodge was equally turbulent. When they divorced in 1879 after five years of marriage, she claimed that Dodge had "treated [her] roughly all the time" and had hit her when she tried to protect her son from Dodge's abuse. Her third marriage, to Henry Brallier, lasted about two years, between 1890 and 1892, and also ended in divorce, with Charlotte claiming physical abuse. Modern historians suggest that Charlotte's experiences as a victim of domestic violence were common in the nineteenth century, when social and legal protections for native women were almost nonexistent.

Finally, at age fifty-two, Charlotte married George Effler, and the mar-riage lasted thirty-one years until her death in 1929. At that time, only two of Charlotte's eight children from her first three marriages were still alive, but she also had three grandchildren, whose descendants still live in Clatsop County.

# Marshall J. Kinney

X

## By Nancy Hoffman

According to his niece, he was "an eccentric old dickens," and Nellie Flavel noted in her diary one Thanksgiving that "MJK inflicted us again this eve-ning." These descriptions hardly coincide with a man who, at the time, owned

Marshall J. Kinney at the 1897 Astoria Regatta.

COURTESY OF THE GEARHART HERITAGE COMMITTEE, GEARHART CITY HALL.

one of the largest canning operations in the world and was surely one of Astoria's greatest visionaries.

Marshall J. Kinney did not start out connected to the sea and salmon canning; his working life began with a career in the family milling business. Born in Iowa in 1847, he traveled to Oregon as an infant with his father and mother, Robert and Eliza Kinney. The family eventually settled in the Salem area and purchased several flour mills. Kinney attended McMinnville College before taking over management of the family business in San Francisco. After his father died in 1875, the Kinney family sold the milling business, and Marshall Kinney began looking for a new opportunity.

He soon learned about the potential for canning salmon in Astoria. In 1876 he moved there with his new wife, Margaretta Morgan, and opened the Kinney Cannery at the foot of Sixth Street.

This was the beginning of the era in Astoria when salmon was king, and business was good. Kinney updated the canning machinery and bought a second cannery in Astoria, two in Alaska, and another in Washington. Ultimately he produced more canned salmon than any other canning operation in the

Northwest. Along with the canneries, he invested in a fishing fleet of 150 boats, employing 425 fishermen during the season and 235 people in the canneries.

Ever the entrepreneur, Kinney wasn't satisfied with the success of his canneries. In 1881, with his brothers William, Lyman, and Alfred, he purchased large tracts of forest and developed a sawmill company at Twenty-Third and Franklin. The Clatsop Mill originally produced up to sixty thousand board feet of lumber a day and employed ninety men. Once the Clatsop Mills Company was established, William Kinney took over as president; once again, Marshall looked for opportunity.

This time he turned to transportation and tourism. In the 1880s, people traveling from Portland to Astoria rode eight hours down the Columbia on a

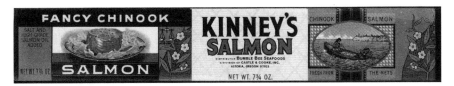

An old Kinney Cannery label later used by Bumble Bee Seafoods, ca. 1960. CCHS 91.070.40.

The Kinney Cannery, later the Columbia River Packers Association, ca. 1893.

PHOTO BY J. H. BRATT. CCHS 274.330.

sternwheeler. If they wanted to continue to Seaside, they climbed into a stage-coach for another arduous journey. Kinney saw a need and joined six other men to form the South Coast Railway. They hoped to build a route from Astoria to Portland that would travel through Seaside and along the Nehalem River. Only the first leg of the project, from Youngs Bay in Astoria to Seaside, was completed, in July 1890. The railway was closely linked to another Kinney project—the town of Gearhart, then known as Gearhart Park.

In August 1890, Kinney purchased a large portion of the donation land claim of Philip Gearhart, three miles north of Seaside. He envisioned a community of beach homes anchored by a large hotel. Realizing that golf was emerging as a popular leisure sport, he also built the first nine-hole course in Gearhart.

Kinney's first wife died in 1880, leaving him with a daughter, Harrietta. He then married Narcissa White in 1889, after unsuccessfully wooing Nellie Flavel.

The photo of Marshall Kinney attending the Astoria Regatta captures a carefully dressed man who could in fact be "an eccentric old dickens." But one cannot miss the shrewdness that made him one of Astoria's most successful businessmen.

# Alfred Kinney

## By Nancy Hoffman

Medical care in the 1800s was risky if it was available at all. Luckily, Astoria was home to one of Oregon's leading physicians, Alfred C. Kinney. When he died, his obituary referred to him as "the grand old man of Oregon medicine."

Alfred Kinney was born January 30, 1850, in Yamhill, Oregon. He attended the Baptist School of McMinnville (now Linfield College) then traveled to New York to complete his medical training at Bellevue Hospital. In 1872 he returned to Oregon and began practicing medicine in Portland and throughout rural Oregon, where he spent the next dozen years. Often he traveled through stormy weather on horseback or by horse and buggy to reach a seriously ill patient or to perform surgery on a family's kitchen table.

Kinney is reputed to be the first doctor to use chloroform to help a woman through childbirth. In 1874 he worked with the Catholic Church to establish St. Vincent's Hospital in Portland, a hospital with fifty to seventy-five beds. He also helped to create the Oregon State Medical Society and served as its first president in 1875. Typhoid fever was raging in Oregon, and Kinney hoped that a medical society would lead to the creation of a state agency that could enforce sanitary conditions. His efforts led to the founding of Oregon's State Board of Health in 1903, and he is credited with bringing the threat of typhoid under control in Oregon. He also helped to establish the state mental hospital in Salem.

ALFRED KINNEY, M. D.
PHYSICIAN AND SURGEON
Graduate Bellevue Hospital Medical College 1872.
Born Oregon, 1850. Address, Astoria, Or.

Alfred Kinney, M.D., ca. 1900.
From *Men of the Pacific Coast 1902–1903*, San Francisco: Pacific Art Company, ca. 1903. CCHS COLLECTION.

Rather than continue as a general practitioner, Kinney chose to specialize in tuberculosis and other respiratory conditions. Moving to Astoria in 1885 and serving as the state health officer for the port allowed him to make the transition. With the move he rejoined most of his eight brothers and sisters, who lived in the area. Kinney practiced medicine in Astoria for the next forty-three years until he retired at the age of seventy-eight, forced from his career by blindness.

While providing medical care in Astoria and serving four times as a member of the State Board of Health, Kinney also became active in the community. He was elected to a term as mayor beginning in 1894, and he also served as a port commissioner. With his brothers, he created the Clatsop Mill, which later became Astoria Plywood and is now the Millpond residential community. As president of the Astoria–Columbia Railroad, he was instrumental in bringing rail service to Astoria, and he was influential in getting channels dredged at the mouth of the Columbia to permit larger freighters to enter.

Kinney died in 1943 at age ninety-three. He passed away in St. Vincent's, the hospital he had helped to found seven decades earlier.

# Narcissa Kinney

## By Nancy Hoffman

The sixth of seven daughters, Narcissa White was born in Pennsylvania in 1854. She worked as a schoolteacher and principal before discovering the Women's Christian Temperance Union, and her calling. Once she embraced the WCTU, she quickly moved from president of the local union in Dover, Pennsylvania, to county president, to state superintendent. In 1880, she became a national delegate responsible for temperance lectures and organizational activities in every state in the union.

Narcissa was a passionate speaker, warning of the mistreatment of women and children and other dangers of alcohol use. She traveled around the country

Narcissa White Kinney, ca. 1880. From *Portrait and Biographical Record of Western Oregon,* Chicago: Chapman Publishing Company, 1904.

advocating prohibition, and she successfully obtained temperance legislation in Oregon and Washington.

According to contemporaries, she was an attractive woman, graceful and dignified, with a clear and penetrating voice. She was one of the most popular and successful speakers in the WCTU. Perhaps it was these attributes that caught the attention of Marshall Kinney during her two visits to Oregon. Kinney was a widower and the owner of one of the largest canning operations in the country. In 1888, Narcissa left the lecture circuit, married Marshall Kinney, and moved to Astoria.

Her energy and enthusiasm did not end with her marriage. Narcissa quickly became involved in Christianizing the cannery workers in Marshall's employ, establishing a mission, and holding services in the cannery. She helped fund and establish Astoria's public library, and she promoted Chatauquas, a forum for lectures and entertainment, throughout the region. Her passion for prohibition led her to speak at many events. In 1894 she was elected president of the state chapter of the WCTU, a role she continued to play until shortly before her death in 1899.

Marshall and Narcissa had no children, but she left a legacy to the area. While she and Marshall were developing the beach town of Gearhart Park, Oregon, Narcissa put a requirement in every deed that prohibited drinking alcohol on the property. Long after Gearhart Park became the town of Gearhart, it remained a dry town. Alcohol consumption in Gearhart did not become legal until seventy-seven years after Narcissa's death.

# Charles William Fulton

X

## By Nancy Hoffman

Just one citizen of Astoria has served in the United States Senate, and that was Charles William Fulton. Born in Ohio in 1853, Fulton began practicing law in Astoria in July 1876. His brother Clyde soon joined him, and later Clyde's son

Left: Charles W. Fulton, ca. 1898. From the Oregon Legislative Album, Session 1899, Salem, Oregon: Statesman Job Office, p. 5. CCHS Collection. Right: Charles W. Fulton was elected U.S. senator in 1903 and served six years in that office. CCHS 17.00F.

Ovation for U.S. Senator Charles Fulton, 1903. At right is the Occident Hotel, formerly located at Tenth and Bond Streets in Astoria. Sovey Collection, CCHS 52.001.049.

joined the firm. Fultons continued to practice law in Astoria and Portland until recently, making the firm one of the longest running family-owned practices in Oregon.

Charles Fulton's interests quickly turned to politics. He served in a number of city offices, including mayor and city attorney. He was elected to the state senate and chosen to be senate president in two different terms. In 1894 he ran for governor but lost. In 1903, the Oregon Legislature elected Fulton to represent Oregon in the United States Senate. Astoria was so proud of this prominent citizen that five thousand people showed up to greet him when he came home after his election.

Fulton's life represents the transition from the Old West of the nineteenth century to the technological revolution that opened up the twentieth. Shortly after Christmas in 1898, an arsonist destroyed a cottage Fulton owned in Seaside, Oregon. The sheriff and many residents suspected a man named Charles Willard, who was thought to be involved in several local robberies. Two days after the fire, Fulton accompanied the sheriff, his deputy, and the local constable to Willard's cabin. All the men were armed, and Willard greeted them holding a rifle. He allowed them to enter and look around, and Fulton recognized some shotgun shells from his cottage. The men questioned Willard about how the shells had come into his possession. He told a story about someone who had just left for Hawaii, then he led them off to look at another cabin.

> *Willard once again rallied and, pulling a gun from his pants, shot three times at the constable, wounding him in the leg. The constable fired back, killing Willard.*

Upon returning to Willard's place, Fulton and the constable went inside to look around again, while the sheriff and the deputy stood guard outside with Willard. Soon Fulton heard shots fired, and he and the constable ran out the back door. As they came around to the front, they found the deputy wounded but struggling with Willard. Fulton raised his own gun and shot Willard in the shoulder. The deputy was bleeding profusely and they didn't see the sheriff, so Fulton told the constable to guard Willard while he went for help. Almost immediately, Willard began grappling with the constable. Fulton returned, raised his gun, and shot Willard in the face. Thinking the man was incapacitated, he left for help. But Willard once again rallied and, pulling a gun from his pants, shot three times at the constable, wounding him in the leg. The constable fired back, killing Willard. When Fulton returned with help, they found both the sheriff and the deputy dead, along with Willard. Only the constable survived the shootings.

A few years after this Old West episode, Fulton was representing Oregon in the nation's capital and driving an up-to-the-minute Thomas Flyer automobile he had purchased for $4,000. (An automobile of the same model would win the famous race from New York to Paris in 1908.) Fulton drove his car several years and then delivered it to the dealership for repairs. Once it had been serviced, the car was to be shipped by train to Astoria. The arrival of a Thomas Flyer in Astoria in 1907 was noteworthy enough to merit a story in the newspaper. Unfortunately, the car arrived with a bill of $994.07. Fulton believed the amount was excessive and paid the dealership only $600. He ended up suing the company and the railroad, while the Astoria sheriff retained possession of the car.

After his U.S. Senate term ended in 1909, Fulton established his residence and law practice in Portland. He died there on January 17, 1918.

# August Erickson

X

## By Amy Hoffman Couture

August Erickson became known for his legendary saloon in downtown Portland. The mahogany bar was 684 feet long, a Wurlitzer Grand Pipe Organ played in the corner, and patrons were sometimes shanghaied. Long before he came to Portland, he had demonstrated his grandiose business ideas in Astoria.

Short and serious looking, with blond hair and blue eyes, Erickson immigrated to the Pacific Northwest around 1880 at age twenty-two. He was a

August Erickson, pioneer Portland and Astoria saloon keeper, ca. 1915.

Finnish fisherman aboard a Swedish fishing boat at a time when immigration from Scandinavia was common, but his downtown business endeavors soon took precedence over fishing. Erickson sold a business on Astor Street in 1894 then hired architect Emil Schacht to design a new building that would become a three-story bar and entertainment hall called the "Louvre." The *Daily Morning Astorian* reported that the saloon at the corner of Astor and Seventh Streets was "fitted up in magnificent style" with elegant woodwork and stained glass. Entertainment at the Louvre included live music, billiards, gambling, a brothel on the second floor, and a skating rink on the third floor. Throughout the 1890s, Erickson leased and purchased other buildings, including a theater next door to the Louvre.

The Louvre Saloon in Astoria, opened in 1896. CCHS 4297.400L.

In 1898, he built a new home in Astoria near McClure School on Eighth Street. In the same period, he operated a roadhouse called the Clackamas Tavern and maintained a separate residence along the Clackamas River near Oregon City. Gustafa, his wife of fifteen years, asked for a divorce in 1899. He complied and moved to Portland, where he soon opened a huge saloon oriented toward "loggers and ranchers, railroad men and miners, fishermen and sailors . . . high and low, adventurers all." Erickson's Saloon on Burnside covered most of a city block between Second and Third and Couch Streets.

*❧ Large crowds of men enjoyed "boisterous and hearty" conversations and "sang the songs of a dozen tongues." ☙*

The saloon was an immediate success. One loyal patron wrote a memoir describing it as a "world-wide rendezvous" where large crowds of men enjoyed "boisterous and hearty" conversations and "sang the songs of a dozen tongues." As many as fifty bartenders worked during each shift, each wearing a white dress shirt, vest, trousers, and a "spic-and-span apron." The saloon was also known for its lunch counter, which offered Scandinavian cheeses, fresh bread, sausages, pickled herring, and lutefisk.

After less than a decade in business, Erickson's livelihood was threatened by Oregon's changing political climate and culture. As early as 1905, many Oregon counties voted for local prohibition, forcing saloons to close or to serve only non-intoxicating beverages. In 1914, Oregon introduced statewide prohibition.

Erickson refused to adapt to the changing times. In 1908, the *Astoria Daily Bulletin* mentioned that Erickson had been arrested for selling liquor without a license at his riverside roadhouse. After gambling became illegal in Portland, Erickson continued to allow it in his downtown saloon, and he was arrested in a police raid. He sold the saloon in 1913 and moved closer to the tavern on the Clackamas, where he continued to sell alcohol illegally.

Erickson's personal life was also troubled. In 1917, the *Astoria Daily Bulletin* reported that Erickson was in jail for assaulting his second wife, Marie, "with intent to kill." While he was in prison, Marie "filed for divorce on grounds of brutality and drunkenness."

In 1920, Erickson was again arrested after police found 130 quarts of liquor at his Clackamas River residence. The *Oregonian* newspaper lamented that he was "once worth an estimated $200,000 [but] has been jailed because he is unable to pay a $150 fine." Erickson lost his Clackamas business soon afterward, and his health began to fail. In November 1924, he was operating a cigar stand in downtown Portland when police discovered "a few pints of moonshine" and arrested him. The *Oregonian* recorded that he died "on a prison cot" at Good Samaritan Hospital in January 1925.

# Jack Williams

## By Nancy Hoffman

Jack Williams arrived in Astoria in 1886. He came alone, with no wife, no family, no relatives to welcome him. New friends in Astoria discovered he was from Kentucky and he had worked for a shoe manufacturer in St. Louis before heading west around 1883. Little else is known about his early life.

Sheriff Jack Williams, ca. 1895, killed by Charles Willard at Seaside on December 18, 1898. CCHS 990.00W.

Williams was said to have a "charming disposition," and soon everyone in town knew him as Jack. He spent some years logging, and his reputation as a courageous and honorable man grew. One year, he and his crew were promised pay at the end of the season. But once the logs were bundled and in the river, no one showed up with their compensation. After the men had waited several days to be paid, Jack became suspicious and decided to camp out atop the log bundle. In the night a towboat quietly arrived to sneak the bundle down to the Columbia. Jack was awakened and refused to move, threatening the towboat captain and crew. Not surprisingly, he was paid the next day. But Jack was not satisfied and refused to budge until the other men were also paid.

In 1896, Jack was elected county recorder; two years later, in June 1898, he won the office of county sheriff by a wide margin of votes. By that time he was in his mid-forties and still unmarried.

Six months later, a Western Union telegram arrived from Seaside, Oregon, at four p.m., reporting that Sheriff Williams had been fatally shot. The telegram identified the murderer as "the desperado" Charles Willard. Within an hour, a hundred men, most armed with guns and rifles, boarded a train to Seaside to seek justice. As the train wound its way from Astoria down to the coastal

Log raft on the Columbia River, ca. 1915. CCHS 6878.630G.

town, another fifty men joined the group. According to the *Daily Morning Astorian* of December 31, 1898, "all were determined that if Willard was still alive, he should be summarily dealt with." A lynch mob had formed to avenge Jack Williams' death.

&#x269C; *"All were determined that if Willard was still alive, he should be summarily dealt with."* &#x269C;

The lynching was not to be. Upon arriving in Seaside, the crowd learned that Willard too was dead, along with a deputy sheriff. As the men gathered around their popular sheriff's body, many were relieved to learn that Jack had died instantly. Willard had fired at him from only ten feet away, driving the ball through his heart. A local constable then shot and killed Willard.

While Willard was unceremoniously dumped in an unmarked pauper's grave, Sheriff Jack Williams was returned to Astoria for a respectful burial and mourned by many friends and neighbors.

# Frank I. Dunbar

&#x2728;

## BY AMY HOFFMAN COUTURE

Astoria's first citizen to win statewide office was Frank I. Dunbar, Oregon's secretary of state from 1899 to 1907. He was long a respected member of Astoria's social elite, despite being charged with embezzlement of state funds in 1908.

Dunbar was born in 1860 aboard a ship on the Atlantic while his seafaring parents traveled to the East Indies. Later he attended school in Brooklyn, New York, and at age twenty-one, he moved to Astoria. For eight years, he worked as a clerk and bookkeeper at A. V. Allen's general store in Uniontown.

In 1890, Dunbar ran for public office and was elected to a four-year term as Clatsop County recorder. In 1894, he was elected Clatsop County clerk, a position he held for two four-year terms. As county clerk, Dunbar streamlined the county's accounting practices with techniques he had learned in the commercial sector. Using new technology such as the "comptrometer," an early type of calculator, he improved the county's financial record keeping.

Dunbar was nominated for secretary of state at the Republican State Convention in April 1898 and elected in November. He took office in 1899, relocating to Salem with his new wife, Lillian Crosby, the daughter of an early Astoria bar pilot. As a child Lillian made frequent trips to visit family in the Puget Sound area, including her cousin in Tumwater, Washington, who would become the grandfather of singer Bing Crosby.

Frank I. Dunbar, ca. 1900. From *Men of the Pacific Coast 1902–1903,* San Francisco: Pacific Art Company, ca. 1903. CCHS COLLECTION.

Frank and Lillian lived in Salem for eight years. During his tenure as Oregon's secretary of state, Dunbar studied law and was admitted to the Oregon Bar Association. A 1907 article in the *Astorian Daily Budget* expressed pride that Dunbar's "service was so creditable" and that he was "never in the lime light of suspicion." His political record was "recognized as an absolute clean one." Yet in 1908, he was charged with embezzling $100,000 in state funds. A lower state court found him guilty, but the Oregon Supreme Court acquitted him.

*He was "never in the lime light of suspicion." Yet in 1908, he was charged with embezzling $100,000 in state funds.*

The embezzlement charge did little to dim his luster in Astoria. In 1908, the Dunbars retired to their home on Harrison Avenue in Astoria and made plans to build a new house at the corner of Seventeenth and Irving Streets. Designed by Emil Schacht, the exquisite home was the site of many social functions, including the Dunbars' fiftieth wedding anniversary in 1939. The *Daily Astorian* reported eighty guests and beautiful decorations at the party, such as "gold and mauve chrysanthemums arranged in tall urns" and "a lovely bouquet

F. I. DUNBAR, Secretary of State.

# State of Oregon

## OFFICE OF THE SECRETARY OF STATE,

*Salem,* January 8th, 1900.

Dear Mr. Carnahan:-

I am in receipt of your favor of the 5th inst., making inquiries in regard to the Articles of Incorporation of the Oregon Pioneer and Historical Society and upon examination of the records of this office, find there were filed therein on May 27th, 1871, Articles of Incorporation of the Oregon Pioneer Historical Society, of which S. H. Smith, J. Taylor, J. G. Hustler, W. H. Gray, A. Van Dusen, John Hobson, H. S. Aiken and T. P. Powers were the incorporators. I enclose herewith a certified copy, which please present to the Society with my compliments.

Thinking the Society might be interested in the proceedings of the Fortieth Anniversary Exercises, which were held in the Hall of Representatives last February, I send a copy of same for its use.

Yours very truly,

Secretary of State.

Mr. R. N. Carnahan, Secretary,

Oregon Pioneer Historical Society,

Astoria, Oregon.

Photocopy of a letter from F. I. Dunbar dated January 8, 1900.

FROM THE ROLL OF PIONEERS RECORD BOOK. CCHS 993.001.

of Talisman roses and gold begonias." The Dunbars raised five children in their Irving Street home.

Frank Dunbar remained active in the community throughout his life. In 1908, he was appointed agent of the State Land Board. He earned a real estate license in 1919 and bought and sold interests in several downtown Astoria apartment buildings. In the 1920s, he was president of the Irving Club, an appraiser for the State Land Board, and a member of the Port of Astoria budget committee. In his final years, he lived within two blocks of many state officials, including three former governors and a U.S. Congressman. Dunbar died in 1945 a week before his eighty-fifth birthday.

# Herman Wise

### By John Goodenberger

When Herman Wise emigrated from Germany at seventeen, it was hardly likely that he would become Astoria's second Jewish mayor. Yet it seemed he became omnipresent in Astoria. According to the *Astoria Daily Budget* of July 23, 1914, "Probably no single individual in the city has been directly identified with more public movements, or contributed more freely toward the public weal.... From a lad he has evoluted into one of Astoria's leading citizens, holding some of the most prominent positions in the community and the very mention of his name can be associated with progress, good cheer, efficiency."

Herman Wise served as city treasurer and as postmaster. A life-long Democrat, he was also admired by Republicans. In fact, both parties nominated him for re-election as mayor. His sense of fairness and his personal generosity attracted people. When Italian stone-masons were on strike at the city waterworks, Wise bucked conventional wisdom and fed them. He liberally gave money, too. In 1899 he

Herman Wise, ca. 1890. CCHS 1371.00W.

Studio portrait of Herman Wise with Seaside,
Oregon, backdrop, ca. 1920. CCHS 128.00W.

maintained Astoria's only baseball team, and the next year he paid all expenses for the city's Fourth of July celebration.

A first-rate clothier, Wise was grateful to his customers for his success. He thanked them with an invitation to an annual ball. One year more than four hundred couples attended the highly anticipated event. If a civic group needed assistance, Wise was ready to lend a hand He helped blaze the roadway up Coxcomb Hill to a city park now crowned by the Astoria Column, a memorial to Northwest explorers and pioneers. On Arbor Day, he helped plant trees in another city park. In 1926, Herman Wise ran a vigorous campaign for county judge. He won decisively, but he did not serve. Five days after the election, Wise died at the age of sixty-four.

# John A. Buchanan

)(

## By Amy Hoffman Couture

John A. Buchanan was an attorney, municipal judge, teacher, army captain, family man, and community organizer, but his passion was writing. He wrote countless poems, essays, ditties, and jingles about the history of Oregon and the North Coast. A portion of one of his poems, "Oregon, My Oregon," became Oregon's state song and was partly inspired by his experiences in the Astoria area.

Buchanan was born in rural Iowa in 1863. His family moved to Monmouth, Oregon, when he was twelve years old. In 1887, at age twenty-four, he graduated from Oregon State Normal School (now Western Oregon University). Moving to McMinnville, he then taught high school for ten years. At the same time he studied law, and he was admitted to the Oregon Bar Association in 1896. He opened a law practice in Roseburg, Oregon, and soon married Madge Ragsdale. The couple had two daughters, Louise and Maurine, who remembered that their father enjoyed hiking, gardening, and tending the roses in his garden with his family. In his spare time, he wrote poetry and miscellaneous essays. In 1909, Buchanan was elected to a two-year term as representative to the Oregon legislature from Douglas and Jackson Counties in southern Oregon.

When the United States entered World War I, Buchanan became a captain in the Coast Artillery and was assigned to Fort Stevens. He became frustrated that the fort

### Oregon, My Oregon

*Words by*
John Andrew Buchanan, 1920

Land of the Empire Builders,
Land of the Golden West;
Conquered and held by free men,
Fairest and the best.
Onward and upward ever,
Forward and on, and on;
Hail to thee, Land of Heroes,
My Oregon.

Land of the rose and sunshine,
Land of the summer's breeze;
Laden with health and vigor,
Fresh from the Western seas.
Blest by the blood of martyrs,
Land of the setting sun;
Hail to thee, Land of Promise,
My Oregon.

did not issue warm clothes and rain gear for his soldiers during the cold and rainy months of their assignment. A local retailer in Astoria generously provided clothing for Buchanan's unit. Buchanan was extremely grateful and soon learned to love the north coast. When the war was over, he and his family moved to Astoria permanently.

In Astoria, Buchanan continued to practice law and became increasingly involved in civic life. He joined the American Legion, the Odd Fellows, the Woodmen of the World, and the Presbyterian Church, and he

Judge John A. Buchanan, ca. 1920.
COURTESY OF CAROL CARRUTHERS LAMBERT.

was a founder and president of the Astoria Kiwanis Club. He worked to identify and preserve local historical sites such as Fort Astoria, the first Custom House, and the first post office. After Astoria's fire of 1922, he and the Kiwanis Club worried that the rock engraved by the shipwrecked *Shark*'s crew in 1846 would be forgotten as new construction changed the city. He arranged to unearth the carved portion of the "Shark Rock" at Thirteenth and Exchange Streets (the rock is now preserved at the Columbia River Maritime Museum).

Buchanan also continued to write. As editor of the Kiwanis newsletter, he frequently published his rhythmic, romantic poetry about the history and geography of the area. Buchanan's poems reveal his love for the Lower Columbia area. In his poem "Astoria," he proclaimed, "No matter where my lot is cast, / or what my fate may be, / my heart turns to Astoria, / Astoria by the Sea."

In 1920, the Society of Oregon Composers held a competition for an Oregon state song. Buchanan won the contest with his poem "Oregon, My Oregon" in combination with the music of Portland composer Henry Murtagh. For several years, the society promoted the song in performances in Oregon's schools and universities, and in 1927, the Oregon legislature voted to make "Oregon, My Oregon" the official state song.

Buchanan died in 1935 at age seventy-two. Just before his death, he spent time at a medicinal hot springs resort in Montana. Here he wrote a final poem in which he anticipated that he would not recover from his illness and wondered what would "lie beyond the Great Divide." Buchanan died as he had lived his adult life, a Westerner to the core.

# Minnie Hill

## By Nancy Hoffman

In the late 1800s, the Columbia River was the main highway for trade with farmers and settlers in Clatsop County. Astoria families would anxiously await ships containing food, dry goods, or mail, then send products back to markets in Portland. Piloting a steam-powered sternwheeler down the Columbia River, Minnie Hill and her husband Charles began their successful shipping business.

Captain Minnie Hill, steamboat pilot on the Pacific Coast, ca. 1886.

Minnie Mae Mossman was born in 1863 in Albany, Oregon. She moved to Portland when she was eighteen in order to teach school, but she soon met Charles Hill. They were married on February 25, 1883. Charles Hill was a licensed steamboat captain. He and Minnie converted an old river sloop to a sternwheeler christened the *Minnie Hill* and operated the boat on the lower Columbia from Longview to Astoria, trading in groceries and dry goods. All along the river, farmers and their wives would meet them. Minnie supplied the women with dresses, hats, and accessories, often modeling them and completely selling out of her supplies. Sometimes they took orders for farm implements, returning with them on the next trip. Other times they would help a family by transporting hard-earned money for deposit in a bank in Portland or Astoria. When the farmers lacked money, they traded for potatoes, produce, and fish.

During this period, Charles taught Minnie to work the engine room, fire the boiler, and pilot the boat around sandbars and snags. Eventually, Minnie applied for a pilot's license at the U.S. Inspector's Office in Portland. Because she was a woman, they refused to let her sit for the exam. Minnie appealed to the San Francisco office, and word came back to Portland that there were no regulations barring a woman from getting a master's license. She then sat for and passed the exam with little trouble. So in 1886, at the age of twenty-three, Minnie Hill became the first woman to receive a master's license as a steamboat pilot on the Pacific Coast. Her original license was restricted to the Columbia River from Astoria to Portland, but it was later extended to include the Willamette River.

*So in 1886, at the age of twenty-three, Minnie Hill became the first woman to receive a master's license as a steamboat pilot on the Pacific Coast.*

Once Minnie became a licensed captain, the Hills purchased more steamers and formed the Dalles–Portland–Astoria Navigation Company. In addition to the *Minnie Hill,* another sternwheeler purchased in 1887 was christened the *Clatsop Chief.* In 1889, they purchased the 111-foot sternwheeler *Governor Newell,* which Minnie captained for eight years. She directed a pilot, a cook, and a crew of deckhands, firemen, and engineers. One of the major projects of the *Governor Newell* was to haul barges loaded with rock destined for the construction of the Columbia River jetties. Minnie was known to tow as many as three rock-laden barges at one time, no small feat.

By 1900, Minnie Hill was thirty-seven and had several children. She decided it was time to stay home and raise her family, so she retired from the river. Minnie died in 1946 at age eighty-three.

# Joseph Riippa

## By Nancy Hoffman

From the time he was a small child, Joseph Riippa had one dream. He wanted to be a minister.

Riippa was born to a large family in Finland in 1867. When he was four, his oldest brother, Jacob, left for the United States. Jacob spent one year in Pennsylvania before arriving in Astoria in 1873. Soon the rest of the Riippas

Joseph Riippa, ca. 1887.

Riippa Collection, CCHS.

followed. Andrew joined Jacob in 1879, and Joseph's father took Charles in 1880. When Joseph was fifteen, he and his mother left Finland for the last time. By the time Joseph reached Astoria, his brothers were settled. Jacob was married and had a daughter, the first Finnish baby born in Astoria.

In 1884, Jacob, Andrew, and Charles decided to homestead across the river in Washington. The brothers obtained parcels of land in the same general area and began farming and logging. Seventeen-year-old Joseph chose not to join them. Instead, he headed east to pursue his dream.

Joseph traveled to Illinois and enrolled at Augustana College, a Swedish Evangelical

Wedding photo of Hilma and Joseph Riippa, 1892.

Courtesy of Matt Mattson. CCHS 5740.00R.

Lutheran Church school. Upon completion of the program, Joseph would have a college degree and become an ordained minister. From the beginning, he was hampered by lack of funds. Letters home to his brothers detailed his frugal lifestyle while pleading for financial support. Joseph supplemented the money his family provided by teaching school and leading worship sessions. When his teaching job became tenuous, he took a job in a department store to secure steady income. He also became active in the local temperance society and led the church choir.

In 1888, four years after he left Astoria, Joseph learned that his brother Jacob had drowned aboard a steamer off Tongue Point when the cargo shifted due to rough weather and the steamer capsized. Saddened by the news and weary of his struggle for funding, Joseph withdrew from college and returned to Astoria in 1889. He went to work for a dry-goods store and joined the Astoria Finnish Evangelical Lutheran Church his brother Jacob had helped to found in 1883. In Astoria he continued his involvement with the temperance society, becoming a member of the band and leading their choir. On November 26, 1892, he married Hilma Lantto. The couple had a son a year later.

*❧ A midwest thunderstorm rolled over the town, and a bolt of lightning hit the church, killing Joseph Riippa instantly. ☙*

Joseph held to his passion to become a minister. In 1895, he and his young family moved east so he could finish his degree. Joseph obtained a job teaching music and English at Suomi College, and the following summer he taught church school to more than a hundred students. He was months away from becoming an ordained minister.

On a Friday afternoon, August 28, 1896, Joseph was sweeping out the church after the students had gone home. A midwest thunderstorm rolled over the town, and a bolt of lightning hit the church, killing Joseph Riippa instantly.

His young widow, Hilma, returned to Astoria with Joseph's body. In tribute to his lifelong dream, he was buried wearing a clerical collar.

# Rose Ingleton

)(

## By Nancy Hoffman

On February 5, 1889, Rose Ingleton shot and killed a man in her bedroom and became the subject of gossip and speculation throughout Astoria.

Rose lived with her husband Jim in an apartment above the Foard and Stokes store at Eleventh and Commercial in Astoria. Married just a year, young Rose wanted to create a comfortable place for Jim to come home to when he returned from fishing each day. One day she asked Neil Livingston, a local handyman, to fix a curtain that hung on the transom over the door to her apartment. Livingston arrived with a hatchet he planned to use as a hammer on the transom. Rose watched Livingston get started then went into her bedroom. She heard the lock on the front door click into place and stepped back into the living room. Livingston grabbed her and pushed her into the bedroom, pinning her under him on the bed.

Rose fought desperately, but she was not strong enough to push the young man off her. Frantic, she thought of Jim and told Livingston that she would shout for her husband if he did not stop. But Livingston knew Jim Ingleton had gone out that morning in his boat. He threatened to cut Rose's throat if she called out and began tearing at her clothes.

Rose remembered the gun, a revolver, Jim often left on the dresser; she was sure she had seen it there that morning. She promised Livingston that she would let him have his way with her if he would allow her to get up and take off her clothes. Livingston rolled off her and turned away. Instantly Rose found the gun, shot him in the back, tossed the gun aside, and ran for the door. But Livingston was not dead.

Enraged, the handyman grabbed his hatchet and chased her. Before she could get the locked door open,

Rose Ingleton, ca. 1910. CCHS 1022.001.

**Hats Trimmed Free !**

This is the lady who sells the finest Hats in Astoria. . . . . A complete line of Ladies' and Childrens' Hats to select from.

**Mrs. R. Ingleton**
WELCH BLK.

Rose Ingleton, featured in an advertisement for hats. From the Tenth Annual Astoria Regatta booklet, 1904. CCHS COLLECTION.

he hit her in the head and neck with the sharp end of the hatchet. Finally she got the door open and burst into the hallway with Livingston right behind her.

Upon hearing the commotion, neighbors in the hallway began opening their doors. Livingston staggered across the hall and fell dead in a neighbor's living room. Another neighbor comforted Rose as blood streamed from her wounds.

*The coroner's report concluded that the killing was justified because Rose defended herself from "an attempt to outrage her person."*

The sheriff was called, and he began his investigation that afternoon. He determined that a scuffle had occurred on the Ingleton bed, that Rose had injuries "through the skin and down to the bone," and that Livingston had suffered a fatal shot to the back.

The coroner's report closed the case by concluding that the killing was justified because Rose defended herself from "an attempt by said Livingston to outrage her person."

# Melville T. Wire

## By Nancy Hoffman

Melville T. Wire was a widely respected landscape artist during his lifetime, and his works still hang in art galleries and private collections. He also served as a pastor for the Methodist Church of Oregon for sixty-one years, including several years in Astoria in the 1920s. The same Melville T. Wire actively supported the Ku Klux Klan (the KKK), chastising Klan opponents from his pulpit in Astoria.

Born in Austin, Illinois, in 1877, Wire came to Oregon in 1884 with his family when his father became pastor of Salem's First Methodist Church. As a youngster, he demonstrated talent in drawing and painting, and he studied art at a children's academy associated with Willamette University until he was sixteen. He also attended the University of Oregon and produced some of his most famous watercolors and sketches during a trip to Bend when he was still a teenager.

Temporarily setting art aside, he studied for the ministry in Illinois and returned to Oregon in 1902 as a fully ordained minister of the United Methodist Church. In the rest of his career, he traveled the state of Oregon preaching and painting.

While traveling and enjoying the outdoors, Wire developed a passion for landscapes and seascapes. He became proficient in several art media, creating many etchings, a few watercolors, and hundreds of oil paintings and pencil sketches. He won special

Melville T. Wire, ca. 1922.
COURTESY OF THE FIRST UNITED
METHODIST CHURCH OF ASTORIA.

recognition for his work from the Oregon Society of Artists in 1931 and 1937, and an exhibit of his work appeared in Salem as recently as March 2005. As a minister he traveled throughout Oregon. His artwork is valued for capturing the diversity of Oregon's environment at a critical time in the state's history. Into his late eighties, Wire continued to draw and paint two hours a day.

His work as a minister brought Wire to Astoria in 1921. In the few years he served as Astoria's Methodist minister, he was involved in two of the darkest events in the city's history.

The more notorious episode occurred during a meeting in the church. On February 1, 1922, James L. Hope, a Catholic attorney, stood up at a gathering of the Astoria Law Enforcement League. Many citizens were concerned about blatant corruption within city government, apparently sponsored by the Klan. Hope complained that the Ku Klux Klan was turning community groups against one another and bringing chaos and corruption to the city. He also complained that he had been defeated in his bid for re-election to the Astoria school board because of his religion.

At that point, Reverend Wire stood up and said, "You can't say anything against the Ku Klux Klan from the rostrum." Other Klan supporters then chastised Hope for raising issues against the Klan while a guest of the church. They noted that the church was anti-Catholic, and criticism of the Klan was offensive to the pastor. Hope apologized for being discourteous and left the meeting. Approximately half the crowd sympathized with Hope's sentiments, but the rest agreed with the reverend, and Wire became a symbol of Astoria's active involvement with the KKK.

*Wire became a symbol of Astoria's active involvement with the KKK.*

The second event occurred on December 8, 1922, when fire destroyed downtown Astoria. The Methodist Church, located at Eleventh and Franklin, was endangered, but Wire joined others on the roof with hoses and saved the building, one of the few structures that survived.

Artist, minister, and KKK sympathizer, Wire moved to Pendleton in 1925 because it was church practice to move ministers frequently in order to prevent political entanglements in the parish. He moved many more times before retiring in 1946, when he settled permanently in Salem, Oregon. Over the years, his artistic accomplishments have become his legacy, and little is recorded of his career as a Methodist minister or his KKK sympathies. He died in Salem in 1966 at the age of eighty-nine.

# Maria Raunio

## By M. J. Cody

Astoria, hotbed of radicalism? From 1904 to the 1940s, the Finnish Socialist Club was one of Astoria's most prominent organizations. According to historian Paul George Hummasti, Finns tended to be more radical than other Scandinavian immigrants and were "one of the largest ethnic groups in the twentieth century socialist parties in the country." As home to the largest settlement of Finns west of the Mississippi, Astoria was receptive to the socialist movement. In 1911 Maria Raunio arrived to add her distinct and voluble voice on behalf of women's suffrage.

Maria Raunio, ca. 1910. From *Muisto-Albumi* by Helmi Mattson, published in 1965 by the North West Historical Society, p. 29. Courtesy of Liisa Penner.

Maria Saarinen was born May 26, 1872, in Keuruu in central Finland. Her father, Erlund Saarinen, was a tailor, and Maria, the oldest of thirteen children, trained as a seamstress. At age seventeen, Maria was chosen as the ideal country girl by Finnish painter Akseli Valdemar Gallen-Kallela, who depicted her in his painting *A Girl in Keuruu Old Church*. Maria would prove the painter wrong, as she became far from the typical country girl. Influenced by radical cobbler Eetu Salin, who spoke against the church as no longer meeting the needs of the people, Maria experienced a political awakening.

Age twenty-one in 1893, Maria married Kalle (Flint) Raunio, a painter from Iittala ten years her senior. (It is unknown why Kalle changed his surname to Raunio in 1889.) In the next eleven years, they had seven sons, two of whom died young. Kalle and Maria became activists in the socialist movement. But work was scarce, and in 1904 Kalle sought employment in the United States. He died in a mining accident before Maria and the boys could join him there. Maria, now a widow with five children to support, worked passionately to promote the status of Finnish women. They gained the vote in 1906, and in the Finnish parliamentary elections of 1907, nineteen women were elected members of Parliament. Finland was the first European country to allow women as governing members.

*Maria worked passionately to promote the status of Finnish women.*

Maria was elected to Parliament as a representative from Vaasalaani, under the Social Democratic Party. She served her two-year term, but was not re-elected due to conflicts among socialists, conservatives, and members of radical right-wing parties.

Maria Raunio, ca. 1908. From *Toveritar Kymmenvuotias, 1911–1921,*
published in Astoria, Oregon, by Toveri Press, p. 10. CCHS COLLECTION.

Maria worked as editor of the newspaper *Raivaja* for part of 1910, but heated conflicts between political parties led her to seek a better life in America. Many members of her minority Social Democratic Party had fled there to "spread the word." In October 1910, thirty-eight-year-old Maria Raunio, a widow barely five feet tall, left her children behind with relatives and sailed for America.

Maria joined the large Finnish community of Fitchburg, Massachusetts. Within months, she married a tanner named Aaltonen. Aaltonen was unable to support them, and they soon separated. In 1911, Maria moved to Astoria, Oregon, as editor of a new national Finnish newspaper, *Toveritar* (The Woman Comrade). *Toveritar* and its counterpart, *Toveri* (Comrade), were products of the Western Workmen's Co-operative Publishing Co., whose purpose was to spread the socialist doctrine. Maria took her new job seriously, admonishing women:

> You, the cradle rocker of society, mother, working woman, you who are the slave of an enslaved slave, you whose burden is two-fold, for whom the cup of life does not sparkle with the intoxicating liquors of happiness and joy, but whose cup contains sorrow. Do you still remain in your stupor! . . . Every working woman must come to understand that the dawning of the new era requires the work of all. . . . The *TOVERITAR* INTENDS TO BEGIN SPREADING THIS MESSAGE NOW!

After only eight weekly issues, Maria Raunio's voice was heard no more. On September 2, 1911, her landlady discovered Raunio comatose in her bed. A few hours later, she died. According to inquest testimony by Aku Rissanen, editor of *Toveri,* since her arrival in Astoria she had been "nervous" and had not slept well. He purchased the sleeping powder on which she, according to the inquest jury, accidentally overdosed. A large crowd attended her funeral.

Maria Raunio's small headstone can still be seen at Greenwood Cemetery. Curiously, above her name on the stone is the Communist symbol of the hammer and sickle with a star. It was probably added after her death, as she was widely known as a Social Democrat—too revisionist and too democratic for Communists.

# Polly McKean Bell

)(

### By Nancy Hoffman

Much of Astoria's heritage, both physical history and written history, exists today through the efforts of Polly McKean Bell and her son, Burnby Bell. A dedicated amateur historian, she was active in both the Clatsop County and the Oregon Historical Societies, and she pioneered in efforts to save Astoria's Flavel House, to accurately establish the site of Fort Astoria, and to locate and preserve memories of Lewis and Clark's Fort Clatsop.

Polly's grandfather, Samuel T. McKean Sr., came to Oregon in 1848 and served as the first representative from Clatsop County in the Oregon territorial legislature. Her mother, Mary Jane Smith, came west as one of the Mercer girls. These were women Asa Mercer brought to Seattle in 1866 to become wives of the early residents there.

Polly McKean Bell in her youth. Genevieve Butterfield Young Collection, CCHS 22198.

But Smith did not stay in Seattle. Instead, she traveled to Astoria to stay with relatives. While living with the Welch family, she met and married Samuel T. McKean Jr. Their daughter, Polly, was born February 17, 1876.

Polly was a gifted student, attending school in Astoria before entering Stanford University. After only two years, she was forced to withdraw from the university when she suffered severe burns in an accident. In 1899, she married Harry Bell at the Grace Episcopal Church in Astoria, then Harry and Polly moved to Seattle, where they lived and worked for nineteen years. In later years they returned to Astoria. After Harry died in 1932, Polly moved between the homes of her son Burnby Bell and her daughter Constance Bernier.

Polly McKean Bell, ca. 1910. CCHS 1010.00B.

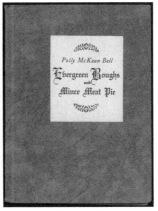

LEFT: Polly McKean Bell in 1962. GENEVIEVE BUTTERFIELD YOUNG COLLECTION, CCHS 22026. RIGHT: *Evergreen Boughs and Mince Meat Pie* by Polly McKean Bell, published in 1952 by Witteveen Press, Eugene, Oregon. CCHS 01.145.004.

Besides working to preserve important sites in Astoria's history, Polly Bell was a prolific writer. She researched and wrote about pioneer days in Astoria, producing articles for magazines and newspapers and a small book titled *Evergreen Boughs and Mince Meat Pie,* the story of a Christmas in Oregon in the 1880s.

When Polly Bell died in 1964, at the age of eighty-eight, the *Daily Astorian* noted that Astoria had lost its oldest native citizen.

# Sam Schnitzer

)(

## By M. J. CODY

Russian immigrant Sam Schnitzer literally went from rags to riches. In 1905 he was knocking on doors throughout the Astoria and Warrenton area asking for rags, metal, and even old fishing boots. Sam's one-man scrap enterprise grew into a steel recycling, shipping, and real estate conglomerate that is now worth billions.

Sam Schnitzer, ca. 1935. Photo by Kay-Hart, New York.

Courtesy of the Schnitzer family.

Sheika (Sam) Schnitzer was the youngest child of Avrum and Tauba Schnitzer, born July 12, 1880, in Troyanuvka, Russia, a small village between Warsaw, Poland, and Kiev, Russia. The Schnitzers owned a gristmill and were by no means the poorest in the village, yet life was hard. By the age of thirteen, Sam left home to work at his uncle Velvel Fuchs' dry goods store in the Mediterranean seaport of Odessa. His exposure to fine textiles and merchandise amidst the lovely seaside homes of Odessa may have set Sam on his long quest for a better life. His uncle Velvel and aunt Netta Fuchs immigrated to the United States in 1898 and encouraged Sam's older brothers and sisters to follow. But Sam, at age eighteen, was conscripted to the army and could not leave the country. Because he was small and frail, his duty was deferred until the Russo-Japanese war of 1904. Scheduled to leave for the Russian Far East, Sam contemplated his options: fight the Japanese, or flee to America and join his family members, who had settled in Portland, Oregon.

"I didn't feel that I wanted to kill any Japanese or have any Japanese people kill me," Sam recalled in a 1935 *Oregonian* article. "I watched my chance, and without consulting the captain of my company, I resigned one night and escaped into Austria."

Scraping together what little money he could, Sam made his way to Hamburg, Germany. He wrote to his uncle Fuchs, who in turn sent $110 for ship fare to New York. The letter ended up in a dead-letter box and eventually was returned to Fuchs. By the time Sam finally received the fare, he had spent four desperate and hungry months as a Russian Army deserter in a strange city full of conmen and thugs preying on those awaiting passage to America. Sam booked steerage aboard the S.S. *Graf Waldersee* and arrived in New York on April 23, 1904, with one penny to his name. With the help of the Hebrew Immigrant Aid Society (HIAS), he was granted immigrant status. Ever frugal and resourceful, Sam worked at a dry goods store then carried bricks for a construction company in New York, earning four dollars a week.

*It cost me $1.50 a month for a place to sleep. No, we didn't have beds; we slept on the floor. I allowed myself five cents for breakfast and ten cents for dinner.*

"Four other young men and myself rented a room at $7.50 a month," Sam recalled in the 1935 *Oregonian* article. "That meant it cost me $1.50 a month for a place to sleep. No, we didn't have beds; we slept on the floor. I allowed myself five cents for breakfast and ten cents for dinner. Out of my salary of $208 for the year, I managed to save $85. I bought a second-class ticket to Portland, arriving here in 1905."

Reunited with his uncle, aunt, brothers, and sisters, Sam worked on a production line at Dornbecker Furniture Company, at a cigar shop, and at a metal shop, where he cleaned lead pipes (mostly sewer pipes). Family lore relates that when he complained about his menial jobs, he was told: "Look, you can't speak English very well. You don't have much of an education. There aren't too many things you can do. So why don't you take up peddling?" Sam took the advice and headed to Astoria.

"I had no money to buy a horse or wagon, so I started in the junk business and was my own horse and wagon," Sam said in the 1935 article. "I bought old sacks, brass and copper, old iron and bottles, and carried them on my back till I got as much as I could carry. Then I would take them to a yard where I stored them. If I bought an old kitchen range or some heavy article, I would wait till I had bought enough to make a load, and then would hire an express wagon to go around with me and collect them and haul them to the dock. I shipped them to Portland."

When he had earned enough money, he wrote to his father and asked him to send a bride, a common practice among Jewish immigrants at the time. Sam was told that Toba Finkelstein was coming, but by the time arrangements were made, Toba was engaged to someone else. Sam's father sent her sister, Rachel, instead. Sam and Rachel, later called Rosa or Rose, were married in 1906 and had seven children. The rest, as they say, is history.

Rising from the humble beginnings in Astoria as a rag and scrap peddler, Sam Schnitzer became a steel magnate and one of Oregon's wealthiest citizens. Because Sam lacked formal schooling and relied on family and community connections in his early, struggling years, he avidly supported education and civic responsibility, especially within the Jewish community. His sons helped the business grow to what it is today.

Sam died in 1952. His generosity and sense of responsibility to community were not lost on his descendants, who are known for their business acumen and civic philanthropy. Faithful to Sam's tradition of hard work and stewardship, the Schnitzer family today donate millions annually to educational and humanitarian organizations such as Reed College, Oregon Health and Science University, Mercy Corps, the Portland Art Museum, the University of Oregon School of Music and Dance, and many charities.*

> *Faithful to Sam's tradition of hard work and stewardship, the Schnitzer family today donate millions annually to educational and humanitarian organizations.*

------

*Sam's grandson Jordan Schnitzer is doubly rooted in Astoria. His mother, Arlene, lived in Astoria as a child when her parents, Helen and Simon Director (of Jennings Furniture Company), bought the Beehive Department Store (renaming it the Metropolitan Store) in the Osburn-O'Brien building at Fourteenth and Commercial in the early 1930s. For a short time, the family lived above the store. Decades later, Jordan joined the committee of the Friends of the Astoria Column and was instrumental in helping to restore the city landmark.

# Anna Bay

⚮

## By M. J. Cody

Throughout the 1920s and 1930s, Anna Bay, with her marcelled red hair and flamboyant clothes, was a striking figure about town. For twenty-two years, Anna Bay managed her own rooming houses, otherwise known as "houses of ill repute." City officials and civic-minded citizens regularly tried to put Anna out of business, but their efforts came to naught.

In the early 1800s, Astoria was a rowdy frontier town with few laws. A new territorial court in 1839 established a system of fees for licenses to sell liquor (though not to Indians) and set a precedent for collecting lucrative revenue.

The working girls of the Savoy Saloon, an early "sporting house" in Astoria, ca. 1900.

Detail of a photo of the saloon's interior. CCHS 30182.400S.

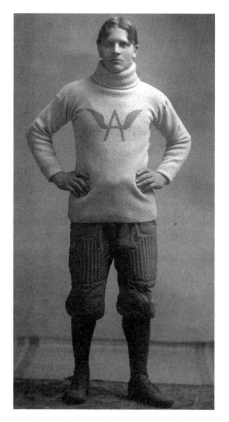

Jack Bay, Anna's husband, in 1903, wearing the Astoria Football Club uniform. CCHS 1139.00B.

The first Astoria town council in 1856 established a city ordinance to collect revenue from the sale of "ardent" spirits. The following year there was an attempt to close "tippling houses" by buying back some of the licenses, but voters favored more, not fewer, liquor licenses. The battle to curtail drink and the attendant evils of prostitution and gambling continued.

In 1878, the *Weekly Astorian* noted that more licenses were being sold even though the town already had thirty saloons. The notorious shanghaier "Bunco" Kelly called Astoria the wickedest city in the world. The same year, Astoria's mayor W. W. Parker, responding to a letter to the newspaper editor calling for the mayor to eliminate public drunkenness and "places of low resort," asked the anonymous writer for ideas on how to manage "500 or 1,000 strong, vigorous, active, young and middle-aged men, fishermen and the like." Parker, like most of the city officials, was unwilling to forgo the profit from licensing fees.

Anna Bay took advantage of the atmosphere that prevailed through the 1930s. Coincidentally, the Parker House Hotel, built, owned, and operated by W. W. Parker's brothers, became the New Richmond Rooms operated by Anna Bay fifty years later.

Mrs. Anna McMillan, age thirty-nine, married thirty-six-year-old Jack Bay in 1920. A year later, Mrs. Anna Bay leased a rooming house over Erickson's Floral on Commercial Street. In October of 1921, the city council refused her license to operate the Imperial Rooms at Sixteenth and Commercial Streets. Three weeks later the license was granted. It is unknown whether Anna as Mrs.

> ## Richmond Hotel Mrs Anna Bay mgr 340 Astor

Anna Bay's listing in the 1931 R. L. Polk directory for Astoria.

A listing also appeared in 1925.

McMillan operated any such "rooming houses," or if she was influenced by Jack Bay, who at one time tended bar and was a well-liked and enigmatic "sportsman" about town.

At age thirteen, Bay was arrested for curfew violation and denied being a member of the "Dirty Dozen," a gang of hooligans. Trouble may have run in the family, as his brother Matthew died in a suspect duck-hunting accident, and his eighty-five-year-old fisherman father drowned under questionable circumstances. According to two Astorians who knew Jack Bay at the time, the union was a "marriage of convenience," primarily a business partnership. After the 1922 fire destroyed most of downtown Astoria, including the Imperial Rooms, Anna again faced legal problems in obtaining a license. As before, she was at first denied a license to operate an establishment, the New Richmond Rooms, in the Parker House Hotel at Eighth and Astor. A month later, her license was granted. From 1923 on, Anna was in business.

*Anna was in business. She was listed as "head of household, house of ill fame." Her "girls" were "chambermaids" or "housekeepers."*

It was said that Anna had the "prettiest girls" and they did not loiter on the street, an indication of a higher class of prostitute. Their working names may have reflected Anna's sense of humor: Rosetta Stone, Daphne, Delilah, Rose la Fleur. Nothing was hidden about Anna's occupation. In the 1930 census, she was listed as "head of household, house of ill fame." Her "girls" were "chambermaids" or "housekeepers." Jack Bay was listed as a dairy farmer in Mishawaka (Elsie) with assets of $10,000—a high amount indeed for a farmer of the era. Anna and her female employees used the farm as a retreat.

In May 1930, Anna, with her young niece, was about to cross a railroad intersection when she saw, too late, a Tidewater Timber Company "speeder" locomotive barreling toward her. Anna put on the brakes, which caused her car to skid partially onto the tracks. The "speeder" threw on its brakes and smashed into her fender. Anna and her niece were fine. But the force of braking catapulted fifty-year-old logger Theodore Karchoff out of the open train onto the tracks, where he was run over and killed. Anna was exonerated in his death. In an unrelated incident three months later, she pled guilty to alcohol charges, was fined $500, and served ninety days in jail. Although the two incidents were not connected, after her jail sentence, Karchoff relatives sued Anna for $10,000 for Karchoff's "wrongful death."

From 1931 to 1937, Mrs. Anna Bay, the "Madame of Astor Street," operated the New Richmond Hotel at 340 Astor Street. In 1938, she moved next door to manage the Rex Hotel at 338 Astor.

Anna was visiting San Francisco in 1938 when a curious item appeared in the *San Francisco Chronicle* under the headline "Nude Woman Won't Quit Bed." Firemen broke into an apartment where Anna was sleeping to put out a fire, but she refused to get out of bed because she was naked. They turned the fire hose on her smoldering bed, and she remained under the covers until the fire was out. Could it be that Anna Bay was bashful?

Jacob O. "Jack" Bay died in 1941 at age fifty-seven. A year later, in December of 1942, pressured by the wartime clampdown on prostitution, sixty-one-year-old Anna Bay sold her summer home near Elsie and left for New York.

One last item in Astoria newspapers announced her remarriage in 1950. A letter in the Clatsop County Archives from Hilda M. Erickson (Mrs. F. C. Erickson) written to a Mr. Welch in Astoria on September 12, 1953, mentions meeting Anna Bay and her husband, Charles Gottlieb, "a lovely gentleman who knows nothing of her past," in Santa Monica, California. Mrs. Erickson describes Anna as being "very domesticated, cleaning the refrigerator" in her apartment. She goes on to write that Anna's husband "is in the lithograph business, a really nice man and they seemed happy."

It is not known where or when Astoria's famous Madame of Astor Street died.

# John E. Wicks

)(

By Nancy Hoffman

Stroll through Astoria, and you cannot help but pass a house or building designed by the architect John E. Wicks. Rather than devote his efforts to a few large or notable projects, Wicks designed as many as 340 structures throughout the area, from homes to schools to commercial properties and churches. Today's owners take pride in proclaiming that they own a John Wicks building.

Wicks was born in Vaasa, Finland, and immigrated to Denver when he was nineteen. In 1903, he enrolled in an architectural program at Bethany College in Kansas. His success is the stuff of legend. Rather than complete the coursework in the prescribed three years, Wicks worked day and night and finished in a single year. It is said he was offered a scholarship to continue his education at Stanford, but instead he chose to establish an office in Astoria, where his brother lived.

Wicks immediately set to work, and he was prolific. Perhaps the oldest of his buildings still standing is the Andrew Young house, which he designed in 1905. He married Maria Cederberg the same year, and they began a family. Eventually they had three successful daughters, Ethel, Esther, and Ebba. Ethel taught school in Astoria for twenty years, and

John Wicks, ca. 1935. CCHS
30948.400A.

151

LEFT: John Wicks at a Clatsop County Historical Society event, ca. 1955. CCHS 28193.
RIGHT: Ebba Wicks Brown, John Wicks' daughter and business partner. CCHS 7833.00B.

The Norris Staples house, Fourteenth and Jerome Streets,
ca. 1985, designed by John E. Wicks. CCHS 5927.960.

Esther taught music. Ebba became an architect and later joined her father in his practice. In 1919, Wicks was appointed to the first Oregon State Board of Architect Examiners, receiving license number 3.

The Otto Owen house, ca. 1980, designed by John E. Wicks. CCHS COLLECTION.

The great fire of December 8, 1922. CCHS 2872.935.

The horrific 1922 fire that destroyed much of downtown Astoria also destroyed many of Wicks' buildings. Along with architect Charles T. Diamond, Wicks was instrumental in rebuilding the city. As many as thirty-four buildings in the current downtown area can be attributed to Wicks' designs.

Astoria High School, 1653 Jerome Avenue, designed by John Wicks, ca. 1910.
Today it is the home of Clatsop Community College. CCHS COLLECTION.

Wicks also designed Astoria High School (currently the location of Clatsop Community College), John Jacob Astor School, and Captain Robert Gray School. He is credited with the Home Baking Company, the First Baptist Church on Seventh and Commercial, and the Lutheran Church on Twelfth and Exchange. He also designed the Finnish Meat Market and the Gimre-Svenson Building. In addition to schools, churches, and commercial buildings, Wicks designed dairies, apartments, granges, and homes, exploring a variety of architectural styles, including Craftsman and Gothic Revival. Two of his churches were designed in the International style. Still, today, they look modern.

# Fritz Elfving

X

### By Nancy Hoffman

At six feet, six inches with a voice to match his height, the Big Swede was the most famous of river captains during the ferry-boat era. Fritz Elfving, also known as the Crazy Swede and the Viking, was born October 23, 1883, in

Sweden. He signed on as a sailor on a square rigger at age fourteen, then spent a few years serving his country in the coast guard. In 1907, he followed two sisters to Astoria.

He tried several occupations, including ship building and carpentry. A salmon-packing company hired him to go to Alaska and build canneries, and he also opened a sand and gravel business with a brother-in-law. His main focus remained Astoria and the Columbia River.

*❧ Elfving recognized the need for a dependable ferry service. ☙*

Crossing the Columbia River from Astoria to Washington was always a major undertaking, but the 1915 construction of Highway 30, the Columbia River Highway from Portland to Astoria, increased the number of visitors to the coast. Watching the movement of people across the river, Elfving recognized the need for a dependable, scheduled ferry service. In 1921,

The *Tourist 1* car ferry on its first trip, May 24, 1921, Fritz Elfving, captain.
The wheelhouse was later removed and used for the ferry ticket office. CCHS 9326.344.

Fritz Elfving at the wheel of the *Tourist 3*, ca. 1950.

COURTESY OF THE COLUMBIA RIVER MARITIME MUSEUM.

he created the Astoria–North Beach Ferry Company and commissioned a sixty-four-foot ferry from Wilson Shipbuilding Company. The cost was $17,000, and he named the boat the *Tourist*. Success was immediate, so he added *Tourist 2* in 1924 and *Tourist 3* in 1931. The third ferry was over 108 feet long and cost $90,000. It was built in ninety days by the Astoria Marine Construction Company, with the Big Swede prodding construction along through daily visits. Once he put the third boat into service, it made ten trips a day.

Elfving struggled for a few years with the ferries getting tangled in fishing nets and going aground because of the shifting river bottom, but his business grew steadily. His success did not go unnoticed, and competition for the ferry business soon developed. A group of businessmen in Washington formed the Columbia Transportation Company and began running another ferry boat, ironically named *North Beach*. Elfving's ferries originated from the foot of Fourteenth Street, and the competitor started at the foot of Seventeenth.

The struggle for dominance heated up in 1931 and became known as the Ferry War. The two companies used a number of strategies to steal business from each other. They employed young men to call out to automobiles and direct them away from the competitor's ferry landing, or they changed schedules with little notice and offered an earlier start. The ferocity of the competition is legendary, including a fist fight between Elfving's attorney and the manager of the Columbia Transportation Company.

The most famous story is well documented. Crowds of Astorians gathered at the waterfront to watch it play out. In August 1931, Elfving's rival obtained the rights to build another ferry dock at the foot of Fourteenth Street. While *Tourist 3* was across the river, they drove pilings effectively blocking Elfving from being able to reach his berth. When he discovered what they had done, the "Crazy Swede" used his boat as a battering ram and knocked out most of the pilings. The next morning, new pilings were driven

*When he discovered what they had done, the "Crazy Swede" used his boat as a battering ram and knocked out most of the pilings.*

that prevented *Tourist 3* from leaving the dock. Once again, with scores of people watching, Elfving's boat repeatedly rammed the pilings and escaped. The famous fist fight resulted when the two businesses went to court to settle the dispute.

In 1933, Elfving won the Ferry War when he bought the other company. He sold the *North Beach* to a company in Portland that turned the boat into a cargo carrier. In 1941, the military bought *Tourist 2* and used it to mine the mouth of the Columbia. The Astoria–North Beach Ferry Company continued its successful business until 1946, when the state of Oregon decided to take over the ferry business. The state purchased Elfving's entire operation for $163,000 and operated the ferries until the 1966 opening of the Astoria-Megler Bridge, which stretches 4.1 miles from Astoria, Oregon, across the mouth of the Columbia River, to Point Ellice, Washington.

Elfving lived in Astoria and remained active in his church and community until he died March 25, 1971, at eighty-seven. His gravestone is etched with a rendition of *Tourist 3*.

# Francis Clay Harley

## By Liisa Penner

Francis Clay Harley was Astoria's choice for mayor for a term starting in 1917. His humor was contagious, and he was confident. He knew the solution to Astoria's economic problems, and he would take action to solve them. A U.S. Navy base at Tongue Point would bring the prosperity the region was due, he said. He would fix the water system, the roads, and the jail. Astorians had found someone who would listen to the common man, who would cut through the bureaucracy and improve their lives. Harley won the election by a landslide and celebrated by throwing a party for fifteen hundred people at the Dreamland Rink. What Astorians got was a mayor who thought he had been elected king.

At the first City Council meeting in 1917, Harley gave notice that he would not follow the usual parliamentary structure of the meetings but would conduct them as he saw fit. "What we want is results—and we want to get them the quickest and surest way," he said. At a meeting a few months later, when City Council member William Kelly expressed his opposition to the lack of regular procedures, he was physically thrown out by Harley's chief of police, Nace Grant, a former bartender and notorious shanghaier.

After the meeting, Mayor Harley and his comrades went to the Liberty Grill, where they became involved in a brawl. Police officers Carlson and Howard arrested the mayor, who immediately fired them. The other principals in the brawl gave notice that they would sue Mayor Harley. Councilman

Photo of Francis Clay Harley from the
*Astoria Budget,* December 14, 1916.
Courtesy of the Astoria Public Library.

This cartoon of Francis Clay Harley appeared in the September 4, 1915 issue of the *Astoria Budget.*

Drawing of Francis Clay Harley from the *Astoria Budget,*
September 4, 1915. COURTESY OF THE ASTORIA PUBLIC LIBRARY.

William Kelly also announced his decision to sue Chief of Police Grant. In a series of court cases, the mayor was accused of assault and convicted on the charges. The brawls embarrassed the community, and in June 1917, the president of the council, C. J. Curtis, asked Mayor Harley to resign. He refused.

Harley left for the east coast on an extended visit. When he returned at the end of July, he gave a stirring patriotic speech to hundreds of local residents. Soon the mayor conceived another reason he needed to be on the east coast. He was present at the first meeting of the council in 1918, appointing police officers and naming the councilmen to the committees. But he took off again for the east coast while others carried on the work of the city.

When Harley's two-year term as mayor ended, he mailed in his farewell speech. The *Morning Astorian* of December 31, 1918, reported that "gambling, prostitution, and bootlegging is going on without practically any check by the officials." New officials finally took charge of the city, while former police chief Grant retired to his country home and former mayor Harley searched in vain for new worlds to conquer.

# Lem Dever

## By Nancy Hoffman

In the early 1920s, the Ku Klux Klan arrived in Astoria in the person of Lem Dever. He succeeded in convincing many citizens that the Klan stood for morality and integrity, a force to drive out corruption in government and business, while he disparaged Catholics and immigrants. His years of influence were few.

Dever was born in Tennessee, the son of a Klan family. He studied law but joined the army in 1917, traveling to Russia, where he gathered information about the Russian Revolution for the U.S. government. When he returned to the States, he took up journalism. Fred Gifford, the Grand Dragon of the Klan, hired him to be the Klan's publicity director in Atlanta. After several years there, Gifford gave Dever the task of publishing a Klan newspaper in the West. Dever arrived in Astoria early in 1922 and began publishing the *Western American.*

A Ku Klux Klan meeting in Astoria, ca. 1922. CCHS 3503.54.

160

It was a time when labor tensions were high and Astorians were concerned about the impact of immigrants. Dever managed to stir up more tensions by blaming the city's problems on Catholics, Jews, and Chinese. Creating his own slate of candidates to run for mayor and city council, Dever used the *Western American* to stir up suspicions about the motives of the opposition. Following his arrival, Klan membership grew to include five Protestant ministers.

Concerned about editorials appearing in the *Daily Budget,* Dever tried to get the editor, Merle Chessman, fired. Chessman should be replaced, he said, or the newspaper sold to the Klan "at the lowest cash price."

**LEM A. DEVER,**
EDITOR

**COURTNEY T. SANDERS,**
BUSINESS MANAGER

(5)

TELEPHONE 73

*Astoria,*
*Ore., U.S.A.*

In the interest of justice and fair play, in the interest of truth and square dealing, I demand that you repudiate the Chessman frame-up of yesterday's issue, and that the lies in it be disavowed.

Give your friends a CHANCE to help build up your paper, or keep that fellow and allow him to continue his mendacious course and we will all join together in building a new one.

SETTERS FOR MAYOR meets the hearty demand of all the people who have been howling for H A R M O N Y. He will make a great Mayor and will be eminently fair and just in all things. He will be nobody's tool, if that's what is wanted. The very scrubs who are howling for "h a r m o n y" and the ones doing and saying things that make harmony impossible.

Truly and sincerely yours,

*L. A. Dever*

From a letter by Lem A. Dever sent to Lee D. Drake, general manager of the *Budget,* dated September 29, 1922. Courtesy of the Astoria Public Library.

Dever also led a group into a WCTU (Women's Christian Temperance Union) meeting dressed in full Klan regalia and donated money to the cause with much fanfare. He used the *Western American* to spread rumors about people in city government and succeeded in driving some people not only out of office but out of the city. He caused the resignation of the president of the chamber of commerce and a respected school-board member because both men were Catholic. In a pamphlet he wrote later, he admitted to using lies to defeat his opponents.

When the November 1922 election results were tallied, the Klan won a complete victory. They had driven out all Jewish and Catholic office holders, including Ed Foster, the fire chief. A month later, a fire destroyed most of downtown Astoria. This fire, a disaster for Astoria, proved to be the end of Klan influence in city politics.

Dever moved back to Atlanta to work directly with Grand Dragon Gifford. From there, he waged a campaign against Astoria's city manager, O. A. Kratz,

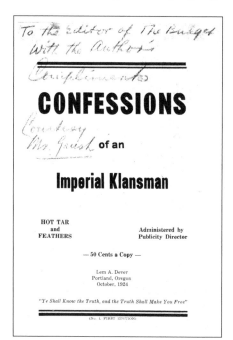

Cover of *Confessions of an Imperial Klansman: Hot Tar and Feathers,* by Lem A. Dever, published in 1924 in Portland, Oregon. CCHS 94.014.006.

through articles in the *Western American.* Pointing out that Kratz's name meant "rats" in German, Dever complained that the man would not appoint Klan members to city jobs and declared him "intransigent."

Kratz, however, was highly competent and able to rebuild the city, hiring people for their abilities rather than their Klan sympathies. The people of Astoria were relieved to see how quickly the town recovered. Klan members on the city council, though reluctant to force the powerful Dever out, began to distance themselves from him.

A man with little loyalty, Dever became angry with Gifford in 1924. He abruptly left the Klan and wrote two angry pamphlets published in

B. A. GRUSH
REGISTERED NEWSDEALER
367 ASTOR STREET
ASTORIA, OREGON

# *Introductory*

I MAY not be the David to slay the Klan Goliath, but, sink or swim, survive or perish, I give my heart and hand to the effort, repairing, as far as possible, the wrong I committed, unintentionally, in promoting this giant fraud instead of opposing it.

My intention is to publish only the facts essential at this time, for a history of the Klan would require a large volume. If the Klansmen persist in being victims to such a fraud and delusion, after they know about it, and if the ex-Klansmen permit reorganization and promotion upon the present basis, now being projected from Atlanta, they will deserve all that is coming to them, plus exemplary suffering.

I have dictated this narrative to my stenographer in one sitting of five hours, without rewriting for literary polish or skill in arrangement. If critics wonder at my style of placing cart before horse, they should make allowance for the fact that I know my audience and am giving them first what they want, namely: A quick, effective legal remedy for the Klan and its evil influence throughout the land.

If my charges against the Klan are true, the executives whom I indict ought to be in the penitentiary; if untrue, I ought to be there, but I swear they are true, in word and spirit.

Proofs will be found herein verifying the general suspicion that Governor Walter M. Pierce of Oregon, Mayor George L. Baker of Portland, and other public officials, have been and are co-operating in certain ways with the Klan executives, and I will show that the latter plotted and started the enterprise of establishing the machinery for a reign of terrorism in the peaceful and splendid State of Oregon, aiming to duplicate, perhaps to surpass, the terrorism and crime which characterize the Klan's activities in Louisiana, Texas and other States.

The reader will be wise to give this booklet a careful study, and, in certain places, to read between the lines. I must, in honor, leave much to the imagination, for I have no intention of violating the spirit of the Klan Obligation.

Copyright applied for

Introductory page of Lem Dever's *Confessions,* in which Dever regrets and vows to fight against the "giant fraud he promoted instead of opposing it." CCHS 94.014.006.

1924 and 1925, exposing the organization's corruption and deception. The pamphlets described how he had manipulated the election in Astoria. Although he was as guilty of these activities as anyone else, he is largely credited with ending—as well as beginning—the short reign of the KKK in Oregon.

# David James Ferguson

By John Goodenberger

D r. David James Ferguson began his Astoria pastorate in 1924 at the First Presbyterian Church. He was a native of England, attended school in Scotland, and graduated from the University of Edinburgh. During World War I, he served as a chaplain for the British Army in France.

Ferguson's skills as an orator were enough to earn him a place in Astoria's history. But his athletic prowess was what truly set him apart. Ferguson had represented Great Britain in the 1912 Olympics, winning the 135-pound wrestling division. He later won the Sandow medal for physical perfection. During his years in Astoria, he did not let his body waste. Ferguson gave public demonstrations exhibiting feats of strength, weightlifting, and calisthenics. Tearing a deck of cards in two was no problem for him. He tore it into eighths—without removing his jacket. Once he jumped into the ring at a Presbyterian "smoker." Rather than wrestling, he bent ³⁄₁₆-inch bolts into hairpin shapes. He did the same with 5-inch spikes. Afterward, he lectured the crowd on physical culture and the value to sedentary businessmen of staying physically sound. In 1935, Reverend Ferguson's early military experience

David James Ferguson, pastor of Astoria's First Presbyterian Church from 1924 to 1937. From *One Hundred Years 1877–1977, First Presbyterian Church, Astoria, Oregon.* CCHS Collection.

David James Ferguson riding a "bucking bronco" for the Astoria
YMCA Round-Up, ca. 1932. CCHS 3760.540.

again proved useful. He became chaplain and first lieutenant of the U.S. Army
Reserve Corps. Though he was beyond the age to serve, the reverend's extreme
physical fitness trumped the rule. The following year, he became one of three
personal aides to Governor Charles H. Martin. His political connections were
invaluable. As a member of the Columbia Defense League, he campaigned
throughout the state to establish a naval base at Tongue Point, just east of
Astoria. His efforts were successful, and the base was constructed in 1939. After
thirteen fruitful years in Astoria, Reverend Ferguson answered a call from the
Presbyterian Church in Albany, Oregon.

# May Miller

※

BY JOHN GOODENBERGER

"I was born here; and I was raised here; and I hope to God to die here." Stubborn, blunt, and usually right, May Miller was a force of nature. She was born in 1894 to August and Mary Alice Spexarth. Her father, who emigrated from Germany, was a merchant; her mother, from England, worked as domestic help for Captain Cherry, a British vice-consul. May grew up in a wood-framed house built in 1852 on the old bank of the Columbia River. Later the family moved to a house on a site that straddled Astoria's business center, Chinatown, and the "red light" district. May developed a toughness, a sympathy for those who were struggling, and a clear-eyed love for the city. During the Great Depression, May's

May Spexarth Miller, ca. 1950. COURTESY OF RODNEY S. MILLER.

166

LEFT: Detail of a photo showing May Miller in pioneer costume, ca. 1965.
RIGHT: May Miller, ca. 1980. MILLER COLLECTION, CCHS.

husband, an assistant bank cashier, was jailed for embezzlement. May raised her three children alone, selling her handmade crafts and family antiques for income. She was never afraid of hard work. Even in her seventies, May claimed she could out-work the younger generation and proved it by chopping down a tree in her back yard. About the young, she scoffed: "They work in a kind of disgruntled way; they're not happy or grateful for work."

*May claimed she could out-work the younger generation and proved it by chopping down a tree in her back yard.*

May always delivered the goods. In the 1930s, when the neighboring Captain Flavel House fell into disuse, May and her children cared for the yard. Following World War II, the county proposed to demolish the ornate Queen Anne–style mansion. May was furious. She led a drive to make three tax-levy elections a success. In 1951, she paid the county $1 to allow the Clatsop County Historical Society to operate the building as a museum. As a volunteer, she helped to keep its doors open.

Thirty years later, May was honored for her tireless contributions to the historical society. Sam Foster, former president of the society, remarked: "There are people who, when they are told the task is impossible, rise to the challenge and overcome all obstacles. May has always been a fighter for a good cause."

With her booming voice, ice-blue eyes, and formidable stance, May got results like no other. But then, it is said, she never gave anyone a chance to argue.

# Joe Dyer

## By M. J. Cody

If you're lucky, you may catch a glimpse of the elegant cabin cruiser *Merrimac* plying Astoria's waterfront. Dubbed the "Million Dollar Yacht" for her quality craftsmanship and innovation in the 1940s, the *Merrimac* was only one of Joe Dyer's creations. Dyer's Astoria Marine Construction Company was widely known for expert design and manufacture of wooden boats ranging from sailboats and yachts to fishing boats and World War II minesweepers.

Joseph M. Dyer was born in 1898 in South Bend, Washington. Joe was three years old when his family moved to Astoria, where his father managed the Clatsop Mill at Scow Bay. Here Joe fell in love with boats, building his first out of a salmon crate. With his early childhood friends Acme (Ac) and Clair Mansker, Joe spent many hours at shipwright Tim Driscoll's boat shop learning building techniques. The

Joseph Dyer, ca. 1965. CCHS 30308.00D.

168

boys' dream of one day having their own boatyard was cut short when Joe's father died. At age fourteen, Joe went to work at the Columbia River seining grounds. He joined the Navy Reserves at age eighteen, just in time for World War I. During the war years, Joe trained recruits on the Washington coast. Afterward he studied mechanical engineering at Oregon Agricultural College (now Oregon State University). As an engineer, Joe returned to Astoria, where he helped design buildings to replace those lost in the disastrous 1922 fire.

Joe and the Mansker brothers reconnected with the intent to make their boyhood goal a reality. In 1924, Joe borrowed $5,000 from his mother to purchase land on the Lewis and Clark River for a boatyard. With a contract for twelve Bristol Bay gillnetters in hand, Joe and the Manskers launched Astoria Shipbuilding. Though active, the company did not have enough business to support a crew of three. Joe used his own boat, the *Kingfisher,* to pick up odd jobs including commercial salmon trolling, towing, and a water taxi service. The partnership dissolved in 1926, and Ac and Clair moved to well-established shipyards in the Puget Sound area. The three remained fast friends all their lives.

Joe then started Astoria Marine Construction Company (AMCCO) at the Astoria Shipbuilding location. He married Genevieve "Geno" Thompson in 1929. The newlyweds lived with Joe's mother for five years until he could complete a house of their own.

In 1931 Joe was hired to design and construct *Tourist 3,* a 120-foot wooden car ferry, the flagship for Captain Fritz Elfving's Astoria–North Beach Ferry Company. Elfving was an impatient taskmaster and wanted his ferry without delay. Joe and his crew built the ferry in ninety days. When asked how that time frame was possible, Joe said, "I'm not really sure. I was so busy." He acknowledged that he had extremely good shipwrights and all were afraid of Elfving, who was at the worksite every day.

> ℮ *Joe and his crew built the ferry in ninety days. When asked how that time frame was possible, Joe said, "I'm not really sure. I was so busy."* ☺

Joe Dyer was an artist and a perfectionist. He had a quick temper—quick to flare, and equally quick to subside. In one incident with his chief naval architect,

A CROD yacht, the "everyman's" sailboat designed by Joe Dyer, late 1930s.

Joe shouted, "Dole, you're fired!" Dole shot back, "The hell I am! I quit!" Joe stomped out of the office, slamming the door so hard the shock broke its window. Moments later, Joe put his head through the broken door window and said to Dole, "Don't forget, Geno's expecting you for dinner tonight."

Despite his temper, he was always fair and considered his crew as friends. He was a casual man, preferring to be called, simply, Joe. He never had a private office, only a corner desk in the engineering department. His only concession to being president of a company employing over a thousand men was wearing a necktie under his bib overalls.

During the Great Depression, Joe figured that those who had money could still buy boats. Why not sell them yachts at reasonable prices? He and Geno visited yacht clubs and took out advertising in newspapers and magazines, promoting high-grade, custom-built yachts with "speed, style and personality." In 1934, the Columbia River Yachting Association in Portland, Oregon, requested the design of a boat suited for the Lower Columbia River. The yacht was to accommodate racing as well as family outings with a galley and room to sleep four to six people, be stable enough to handle tides and storms, and have a shallow draft to avoid sandbars. Joe loved the challenge. Who better to design such a sailboat than the kid who grew up in Astoria? The result was the twenty-eight-foot Columbia River One Design, known as the CROD. The "everyman's" sailboat was an immediate success. Classic yachts such as the *Merrimac* (originally the *Marymack* after the first owner's daughters) soon followed.

*The result was the twenty-eight-foot Columbia River One Design, known as the CROD. The "everyman's" sailboat was an immediate success.*

During World War II, U.S. Navy designers were interested in developing wooden minesweepers. Joe flew to Washington, D.C., in 1941 to see if he could land the contract. AMCCO had only enough money for one-way airfare. If they got the contract, Joe could fly home; if not, he would return by train or bus. AMCCO's chances were slim. The company was located in a virtually unknown small town and was competing with large shipyards on the eastern seaboard. When Navy Captain Phillip Lemlera asked questions about his company's capability, Joe adamantly responded, "I've got men who can build boats in their sleep."

The contract was awarded to AMCCO.

After the end of the war, Joe realized that AMCCO could do fine without his daily presence and turned to other interests. He had always been involved in community activities, especially the Astoria Regatta, and was passionate about state politics. He ran for the Oregon State Legislature and served two terms, from 1948 to 1952. Joe later became the first chairman of the Oregon State Marine Board. He was also a founding member of the Columbia River Maritime Museum.

Wooden shipbuilding was destined to end, as forests no longer produced wood with the tight, straight grain necessary, and steel and fiberglass became the materials of choice. After nearly forty years, Joe turned AMCCO over to a group of his employees.

Joe died in 1974 at age seventy-six. His son Tom continued his father's legacy, engineering and constructing steel, wood, and aluminum boats. Today, Tom heads a marine consultancy firm, Headway Marine, LLC, in Seattle, Washington. Some of Joe's yachts can still be seen cruising waterways all over the United States. Most of the CRODs have survived. Two can be seen at the Columbia River Maritime Museum in Astoria.

# Rolf Klep

X

## By Nancy Hoffman

Rolf Klep began life in Astoria, became a distinguished graphic illustrator in New York City, then returned to Astoria and dedicated the last twenty-five years of his life to founding and directing the Columbia River Maritime Museum.

Klep was born February 6, 1904, in Portland. His family soon moved to Astoria, where his father was a tallyman for a lumber mill. By age fourteen, he secured a summer job as a deckhand and relief helmsman for the ferry boat *Tourist 1*. Even as a child, he was a prolific artist, capturing images of the ships and sailboats that plied Astoria's waters. After graduating from Astoria High School, Klep entered the School of Architecture and Allied Arts at the University of Oregon, but his love of drawing led him to switch to a degree program in fine

Rolf Klep at his desk, 1960s. *Daily Astorian* Collection, CCHS.

arts. Throughout college, he used his skills as an architectural draftsman and artist to get summer jobs, and he was art editor of the college yearbook. He also took courses in advertising layout and copywriting. Upon graduation, he became a freelance commercial artist in Portland.

In 1929 he married his college sweetheart, Alice Latture, and they began a car trip east so that Klep could attend the Art Institute of Chicago. When they left Portland, they had enough money invested to pay for his education. But by the time they reached Chicago, the stock market had crashed, and Klep had only forty dollars left. His education would have to wait. Instead, he took a job as a commercial artist for an advertising studio.

Klep was an immediate success. He was the first artist in the United States to use airbrushing as a technique in illustrations for advertising. With his skill and reputation growing, Klep and his wife moved to New York City. Because of his love for boats, he particularly enjoyed illustrating brochures for the great steamship lines. He also expanded from advertising to producing technical illustrations in magazines. His work appeared in major magazines including *Life, Look, Newsweek, National Geographic, Better Homes and Gardens,* and *Yachting.* In

1937, he entered the field of book illustration, where he specialized in technical cutaways and focused on children's books.

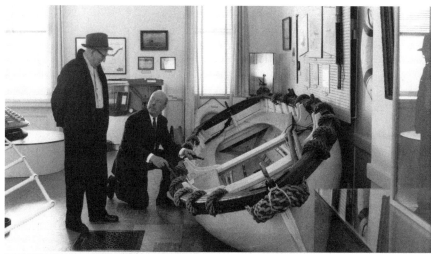

Top: Rolf Klep and a visitor examine a boat at the Columbia River Maritime Museum (now the Heritage Museum), ca. 1970. Courtesy of the Columbia River Maritime Museum. Bottom: Rolf Klep consulting with Michael Naab, curator of the Columbia River Maritime Museum from 1971 to 1980 and director of the museum from 1980 to 1986, ca. 1970. Courtesy of the Columbia River Maritime Museum.

Shortly after the Japanese attack on Pearl Harbor in 1941, Rolf Klep joined the U.S. Navy. The military took advantage of his drawing skills, putting him to work as an illustrator for the Division of Naval Intelligence. His job was to graphically render ships and aircraft for training manuals.

After the war, he returned to New York. In 1952, Viking Press hired him to provide technical illustrations for two books written by Dr. Werner von Braun and other scientists who were trying to explain the complexity of man's efforts to travel to the moon and to explore outer space. The first book was titled *Across the Space Frontier;* it was followed by *Conquest of the Moon.*

Portrait of Rolf Klep as a young naval officer, oil on canvas, ca. 1944.
COURTESY OF THE COLUMBIA RIVER MARITIME MUSEUM.

FORT CLATSOP 1805·06 WINTER QUARTERS of LEWIS and CLARK EXPEDITION

Rolf Klep's drawing of Fort Clatsop, the 1805–1806 winter quarters of Lewis and Clark's Corps of Discovery, ca. 1956. CCHS 23909.796.

Klep is noted for the accuracy of his depictions, created years before man actually walked on the moon or experienced weightlessness.

In 1956, after a hugely successful career, Klep and his wife left New York and returned to Astoria. They settled in Surf Pines, just south of Camp Rilea, but Rolf Klep did not retire. He immediately immersed himself in local activities, serving on the first planning commission and rendering detailed drawings of the 1955 Fort Clatsop reconstruction.

*At least one fellow, worn down after hearing the plea many times, opened his checkbook in exasperation and said, "How much do you want?"*

Then, in 1962, he joined with several friends and began work on the Columbia River Maritime Museum. He was a relentless fund-raiser. The story is that he would haunt the round table at the Arlington Club in Portland, where he pressed his case on anyone nearby. At least one fellow, worn down after hearing the plea many times, opened his checkbook in exasperation and said, "How much do you want?"

Rolf Klep donated books and artifacts from his private collection and served as founder, benefactor, and director for eighteen years, helping the museum become a premier maritime museum on the West Coast. He died on September 13, 1981.

# Burnby Bell

)(

## By M. J. Cody

*If we're going to build the thing, let's make it last fifty years.*

This was the mantra of the dedicated cadre of volunteers who built the first replica of Fort Clatsop in 1955. They did build it; and it did last—fifty years. Burnby Bell, president of the Clatsop County Historical Society at the time and stalwart enthusiast for the project, was not around to see the fort burn to the ground in 2005,* though he did see his beloved fort become a national park in 1958.

Historian and civic leader Burnby Bell devoted decades to preserving the history of Astoria. Bell was heavily influenced by the fervor of his mother, Polly McKean Bell, who at one time in the 1950s admonished citizens in an article in the *Daily Astorian:* "If there had been a conspiracy for fifty years to eliminate Astoria's historical sites and relics, a better job couldn't have been done than has been accomplished through carelessness and negligence of Astorians."

Burnby Scott McKean Bell was born in Seattle in 1905. His names represented his family line. The McKean name was well known in Clatsop County: fourteen family members had settled in the area, the first arriving in 1848.

Following in his mother's footsteps, Bell attended Stanford University. But he left to become the family's major breadwinner after the lucrative Seattle rock quarry business of his father, Harry Bell, collapsed. Harry Bell's partners appropriated all funds and fled to Mexico, financially and emotionally devastating the family.

> ℰ *Historian and civic leader Burnby Bell devoted decades to preserving the history of Astoria.* ℐ

Polly McKean Bell's passion for uncovering history may have influenced her son's inquisitive nature. In the 1930s, after his father's death, Bell moved the family to Portland, where he became an investigator for a large insurance agency. He was now taking care of his mother, his sister, and his sister's son, Harry Bernier.

Although he was nearly forty years old, Bell enlisted in World War II and was stationed in Texas working for the Office of Strategic Services (the OSS), an early incarnation of the F.B.I. After the war, he returned to Astoria to join his family, who were living with McKean relatives.

Bell married Anna Louise "Pinky" Reid Carlson in 1950. "Pinky," so nicknamed because of her red hair, was born in Kalama, Washington, where her father and mother operated a ferry that crossed the Columbia to and from

---

*The first replica of the fort burned in October 2005, a few months before Fort Clatsop's two-hundredth anniversary. Through monumental volunteer efforts, a second replica was built by December 2006.

Burnby Bell with the skull of Chinook Chief Comcomly, March 1, 1953.

CCHS History Scrapbook.

Goble, Oregon. Athletic by nature, Pinky startled passengers who spied the little girl swimming alongside the ferry. When they married, Pinky was a thirty-five-year-old widow with a three-year-old son, Edwin Carlson (named after his father). Their own son, Thomas McKean Bell, was born in 1952.

Also in 1952, Burnby Bell read an account in the *Oregon Historical Society Quarterly* about the graveyard theft of Chinook Chief Comcomly's skull. Englishman Meredith Gairdner had absconded with the skull in the 1830s and sent it to England. The skull ended up in storage and remained there for more than a hundred years. Bell wrote to the director of the Royal Naval Hospital in Gosport, England, to request that the skull be returned to Astoria. Before Christmas of the same year, Comcomly's skull was returned to Astoria and on display in the newly renovated Flavel House Museum. Because of Bell's successful repatriation effort, the Chinook tribal association made him an honorary Chinook member, one of the proudest moments of his life. The skull of the tribal leader was given a proper Chinook burial.

In 1960 Bell began a career with the National Park Service as Historian at Fort Clatsop National Memorial Park. He was responsible for planning the interpretive development of the park and for cultivating historic displays. By 1964, Bell was recognized as a foremost authority on Fort Clatsop and given the Department of Interior Meritorious Service Award in recognition of exemplary leadership and accomplishments in the field of historical research and interpretation.

Burnby Bell died in May 1968, at age sixty-two.

# Emil Richard "Dic" Nivala

)(

## By Nancy Hoffman and Liisa Penner

Emil Richard Nivala, known as "Dic" by family and friends, might more appropriately have been called the Traveling Finn. Born February 7, 1909, in Astoria, Nivala is famous for two unusual journeys.

As a child, Nivala dreamed of visiting the places he saw in his schoolbooks. By 1932, he had made it as far as Los Angeles, California, where he operated a sign-painting shop.

Business had slacked off during the Great Depression. Eventually Nivala was forced to close up shop. All he had left was one penny. Noting the words "In God We Trust," he decided to set off on an adventure with a penny and a prayer. The world faced grave social and economic problems, and he would help to solve them by carrying messages to people everywhere of "understanding,

Dic Nivala with his "Around the World on a Penny" traveling outfit, 1930s.

NIVALA COLLECTION, CCHS.

kindness, goodwill and international peace." He would serve as "Ambassador of the World."

Nivala began his journey at Astoria, Oregon, on July 18, 1932, at age twenty-three. Besides the penny, his only possessions were a briefcase with a world map, a diary, and a change of clothes. The briefcase proudly proclaimed his endeavor on its side so that people he encountered could donate to his cause.

He traveled by "the ankle express" and "the thumb express," walking and thumbing rides. In Salem, he visited the governor of Oregon, explained his mission, and received from him a letter of introduction marked with an impressive gold seal. He collected such letters in a scrapbook he planned to carry around the world to record his impressions and accomplishments.

*He traveled by "the ankle express" and "the thumb express," walking and thumbing rides.*

Hitchhiking to Seattle, Nivala was a passenger in a truck that drove off the road, and he received a head injury. When he awakened, he was blind and deaf. After two weeks in the hospital, he recovered his sight. He continued his journey down the Oregon Coast Highway, nearly drowning in the ocean along the way. As he recovered consciousness, his hearing suddenly returned. He found passage in another truck, this time with a drunk Italian rancher who was seeing two roads instead of one. After another accident, he quickly recovered.

Nivala went south through San Francisco to Hollywood, talking to anyone who would listen to him and writing several articles to raise funds. With that money, he traveled to Mexico and visited thirty-eight states. Everywhere he went, he searched out the people he admired and called upon them. Upton Sinclair gave him a letter of introduction that he proudly added to his scrapbook. A few weeks later, he visited with Edgar A. Guest. Newspaper articles fill his scrapbooks, which are held by the Clatsop County Historical Society.

In August 1933 he arrived in New York, where he talked a ship officer into giving him free passage across the Atlantic in exchange for keeping tabs on two suspicious passengers. By this time, he was wearing his original penny on a string around his neck.

In Finland, he visited his father's native village of Rautio. He finagled free boarding with two college students in exchange for English lessons. He also talked a theater owner into showing a children's movie and charging a broken toy for the price of admission. Someone else donated paint, tools, and a workshop where he repaired the broken toys. He then helped distribute the toys as

Christmas gifts for needy children. This activity brought in no money, so he also gave lectures about his travels, which earned him enough money to eat.

In September 1934, more than two years after he left Astoria, Nivala arrived in England on a Finnish steamer. He stopped in London and called on Lady Astor. He again earned money talking about his trip, and he expressed plans to continue his travels for six more years and to visit Egypt, India, and Australia. He visited Paris; later he went to Nice and Monte Carlo, places he described as the "weeds of evil that must be uprooted by the coming generation." He was refused admittance to Switzerland for lack of funds and had to return to France. He scrawled in his scrapbook: "Wet, tired and hungry near a mountain village in France where I do not understand them . . . but I must smile and march on, on and on, wondering what tomorrow holds."

Deciding to cut his journey short, he left Europe for the Panama Canal and traveled north through Central America. More than a hundred thousand miles later, he arrived back in Astoria in July 1935, talking about the ominous clouds of war over Europe. He had come home with his original penny and "a million dollars worth of fun," as he described his travels in a 1941 KOIN radio interview.

In 1939, at age thirty, Nivala decided to run across the United States, from Seaside, Oregon, to New York City. It took less than three months. At first he ran twenty-five to fifty miles a day. When he reached Gary, Indiana, he heard that the Russians had invaded Finland. From then on, he averaged seventy miles a day,

Dic Nivala in Finnish military uniform, ca. 1940. Nivala Collection, CCHS.

Dic Nivala, ca. 1960.

NIVALA COLLECTION, CCHS.

arriving in New York just in time to board a ship of U.S. and Canadian volunteers heading to Finland to join in the fight. By January 12, 1940, he was a member of the Finnish Army.

Nivala later served in the U.S. Navy, where he earned the Silver Star, then joined the U.S. Merchant Marine. After World War II, he settled in California, where he worked for the Hollywood Foreign Press Association for twenty years. In 1978 he was awarded the Order of Knighthood of the White Rose of Finland because of the aid he had provided that country almost forty years earlier. Dic Nivala died February 11, 1991, in California.

# Helmi Huttunen Mellin

)(

## By Liisa Penner

Eccentric people can hide anywhere—in a perfect mother straight out of a 1950s sitcom, for instance, or a dedicated businesswoman. My mother, Helmi Huttunen Mellin, was never anything like the mothers my sister and I saw on television in our teens and twenties. We saw her as a person whose life completely revolved around her "hole in the wall" restaurant.

In the 1950s, she was running her own restaurant in Astoria and was her own boss after years of servitude cooking for wealthy families on both the east and the west coasts. Now, instead of making dainty tea sandwiches and petit fours, she was making Finnish-style fish stew and flatbread. Instead of serving Mr. and Mrs. at their candelabra- and lace-decorated table, she filled coffee cups up and down her counter and bandied jokes with the crew from the ferry landing and the auto mechanics who worked nearby. If a customer at her restaurant

Helmi Mellin in Finland, 1940. Courtesy of Liisa Penner.

demanded coffee "Now!" she didn't hesitate to reply, "Get out! And don't come back!"

Helmi was born in 1909 on a small farm in central Finland. Her father made the shoes she wore. She made her own clothes from flax they grew in their field and soaked in the lake until the outer sheaf rotted; she wove the remaining fibers on a loom. Envisioning a life as a drudge on her parents' farm, she schemed to come to the United States.

Helmi and her neighbor, Hilda, borrowed money to get themselves to Toronto, Canada. They arrived in 1929 with $5.00 between them and

Helmi Mellin at Hermosa Beach in California, ca. 1950. Courtesy of Liisa Penner.

no English-language skills. At first, they worked for families in Toronto. Then one night Helmi, eager to see the United States, crossed the border into New York and found work under an assumed name, as an illegal immigrant.

After almost a year of working for a wealthy couple and being called by the assumed name, one night she impulsively blurted out: "Stop calling me that! My name is Helmi!" The couple urged her to turn herself in to the authorities after she told them what she had done. She was sent back to Finland, but a couple of years later she returned after being sponsored by the same family. Helmi worked as a cook for this family as well as others in New York. This time she was a legal visitor; later she became a citizen.

In 1940, when Russia was raining bombs on Finland, my mother pictured the hardships her relatives were facing. Along with other Finnish Americans, she boarded a ship for Finland to join in the war effort. All were eager to help, whether or not they survived the war.

When she returned to the U.S. a year later, Helmi came with a husband and a baby. Her husband wasn't Finnish but had joined in the war effort. A second child, Karen, was born in Chicago in 1942. The family then moved to southern California, where her husband worked in the shipyards as a pipefitter and welder. For a brief four or five years, she relaxed on the beach in California

with two children in sunsuits. Her leisurely life ended when her husband abandoned her. The children were placed with other families, and Helmi again became a live-in cook.

On a trip to Astoria in 1951 with her old friend Hilda, Helmi fell in love with a restaurant. She became part owner; a couple of years later, she became full owner. For the twenty-seven years she owned the restaurant, no one dictated to her. She was free.

Top: Helmi Mellin at her kitchen table, ca. 2005. Courtesy of Liisa Penner.

Bottom: Helmi Mellin in her restaurant, Koffee Kup, in Astoria. Cartoon by Hal Allen, ca. 1978. Courtesy of Liisa Penner.

# Edward Harvey

X

D r. Edward Harvey was born in 1911 in Amherst, Massachusetts. He was the director of the local Food Products Laboratory, specializing in seafood. Later he co-founded the Oregon State University Seafood lab in Astoria. Although he was well respected as a professional, he was best known for pioneering the historic preservation movement in Astoria.

Dr. Edward Harvey, 1969. Ball Studio Collection, CCHS.

In 1944, he and his wife Ruth purchased the J. D. H. Gray house, a circa 1880 Italianate-style residence. In renovating, they paid little heed to accurate historic detailing, but decorated the interiors to suit their own tastes. Dr. Harvey's East Coast roots emerged in details more appropriate to a Colonial Williamsburg Revival than to a West Coast Victorian. American eagles, symbols of patriotism, appeared on curtains surrounding tall windows and in full relief above doorways.

In the 1960s, Harvey's neighborhood, along with most of Astoria, was suffering from neglect. Many older homes were in desperate need of repair. The city's solution was to begin a demolition program. Dr. Harvey's solution was to educate the public to the value of Astoria's historic structures.

Using old highway signs as a canvas and hand-painted calligraphy as his medium, Dr. Harvey wrote brief histories of particular houses. He presented the recycled signs to homeowners of his choosing. Signs appeared throughout the city, mounted on the walls of residences, on fences, on prominent posts. It was

Dr. Edward Harvey owned and renovated the J. D. H. Gray house at 1687 Grand.
His characteristic sign of approval can be seen at front right. CCHS 4116.96.

said that Dr. Harvey kept a watchful eye on his chosen houses. If property owners painted the house in colors he disliked, their historic plaque might disappear in the night.

Today the City of Astoria officially recognizes Harvey's efforts. Each year, the Historic Landmarks Commission presents the Dr. Harvey Award for excellence in preservation. In the beginning, the awards went to people who simply took the time and trouble to paint their house. Now the award is frequently given to owners who have accomplished a complete, painstakingly accurate restoration of their historic property.

Dr. Harvey's plaques are coveted to this day. Their very presence on a building testifies to its historic importance and helps to ensure that it will be maintained and preserved for the future.

# Edgar Quinn

X

## By Nancy Hoffman

The lure of the sea called to Edgar Quinn his entire life, a siren's song he could not resist.

Quinn was born August 26, 1911, in New York, but he grew up in England. He returned to the United States when he was eighteen, going to work for the United Fruit Company as a sea cadet. Checking cargo and maintaining the ship's bridge and wheelhouse, Quinn worked long hours for little pay. Through practical experience, he hoped to pass the exams for ship's officer.

After he received his training with the UFC, he became a seaman for the American President Line, a steamship company that operated across the Pacific and around the world. He was

Captain Edgar A. Quinn, ca. 1965. BALL STUDIO COLLECTION, CCHS.

assigned to work in the forecastle. Then, in 1936, Quinn became a licensed officer with Matson Navigation Company. During this era, Matson opened up much of Hawaii to the tourist trade with its famous white ships such as the *Lurline* and the *Monterey*. By 1940, Quinn had advanced to master seaman.

World War II caused a break in Quinn's service with Matson, but he continued to sail the seas. Drawing upon his training, he commanded troop ships in both the Pacific and the Atlantic theaters. Following the war, he returned to work with Matson until 1951, when he moved to Astoria and became a Columbia River bar pilot. Although his active military service was over, he remained in the naval reserve until he retired as a lieutenant commander with nineteen years of service.

Quinn showed a deep commitment to Astoria, working with the Clatsop County Library Board, the Rotary Club, the Oregon Historical Society, and the Columbia River Maritime Museum. He married B. J. Christensen, with whom he had two sons and two daughters. Over two decades, he was an enthusiastic bar pilot.

*❧ Quinn and the other survivor lashed themselves to the boat while it overturned several times. ☙*

But the Columbia River is a dangerous place for men who love and work the sea. Quinn barely escaped his first deadly encounter. He was fishing off the bar in 1962 when he and two other men in a sixteen-foot fiberglass boat were swamped in rain squalls and sixty-mph winds. One of the men died of exposure, but Quinn and the other survivor lashed themselves to the boat while it overturned several times. Finally they were able to row the boat through breakers and take it ashore in Westport, Washington, forty miles from where they had started.

Edgar Quinn's luck ran out in March 1973. After he successfully piloted the log ship *Maritime Queen* across the bar, he lost his footing while trying to return to the boat that would take him to Astoria and fell into the ocean. The crew of the pilot boat quickly located him and waited with him until a Coast Guard helicopter arrived, but it was too late. At age sixty-one, Edgar Quinn drowned in the waters that had been his life.

# Sam Churchill

)(

## By Nancy Hoffman

In 1986, while he prepared to narrate his video *Steam Whistle Logging*, Sam Churchill described the speed with which the vast old-growth forests disappeared. "In less than a lifetime," he wrote, "steam power and the logging railroads

Sam Churchill at the controls of a railroad engine, ca. 1965. Sam Churchill Collection, CCHS.

were gone. The diesel engine and the log truck had taken over. The timber and the equipment were smaller. Those giant old growth trees of a century ago were virtually gone." Sam Churchill died in 1991. His legacy lives in his writings and in the video.

Churchill was born in 1911 in Astoria's old St. Mary's Hospital, which was on Sixteenth Street between Duane and Exchange. His father was a logger for the Western Cooperage Logging Company, and Churchill spent his childhood in logging camps. His mother decided her son needed a more formal education than the one provided in one-room schools set up by the logging company, so she took him to Seaside, Oregon, for high school. He later attended the University of Oregon and worked in a variety of jobs, including a stint as a logger. He married his wife, Dorothy, in 1940, and served as a radio technician aboard a submarine tender during World War II. In 1951, he began work as a newspaper reporter and columnist for the daily paper in Yakima, Washington,

*"In less than a lifetime . . . those giant old growth trees of a century ago were virtually gone."*

Sam Churchill in 1972. SAM CHURCHILL COLLECTION, CCHS.

a job that turned into a twenty-three-year career.

While in Yakima, Churchill began working on a manuscript describing life in the logging camps around Astoria early in the twentieth century. Doubleday published his work in 1965 under the title *Big Sam,* a reference to his father's nickname.

After Churchill retired from the newspaper in 1974, he and Dorothy moved the family to Astoria, where he became active in the community. He regularly

Sam Churchill with his book *Big Sam* in 1965. SAM CHURCHILL COLLECTION, CCHS.

contributed time and energy to the Clatsop County Historical Society and the Maritime Museum.

In 1977, Doubleday published a sequel to *Big Sam,* a book titled *Don't Call Me Ma* in which Churchill focuses on the lives of his mother and the other women in the logging camps. Then, in 1986, Churchill helped produce the video *Steam Whistle Logging,* serving as both narrator and interviewer. This oral history documentary captures the amazing speed with which the old-growth timber was removed and logging in Clatsop County changed forever.

# Wally Palmberg

## By Nancy Hoffman

Walter "Wally" Palmberg, ca. 1995. *Daily Astorian* Collection, CCHS.

When Wally Palmberg neared eighty years of age, he regularly walked three miles through his Astoria neighborhood. Each time he passed his driveway, he added a pebble, until he had enough pebbles to represent six half-mile loops. During his walk, he would chat with newcomers to the neighborhood who had no idea that the tall, elderly man was an Astoria legend.

Palmberg was a genuine Renaissance man. He blended athletic prowess with intellectual curiosity and acumen. Five feet, eleven inches tall, he was a basketball wizard. His skill on the court earned him places in the Astoria High School Hall of Fame, the Oregon State University Athletic Hall of Fame, and the Oregon Sports Hall of Fame. In high school, he was the star forward on two state championship teams, in 1930 and again in 1932. At OSU, he became an All-American and All–Pacific Coast Conference selection in 1936, setting scoring records in the process. After

Top: Astoria High School state basketball champions in 1941. Coach Palmberg is at left. CCHS 11742.504. Bottom: Wally Palmberg, at right, with cutouts of the 1942 Astoria state basketball champion squad. CCHS 17737.504.

college, he coached his Astoria team to two more state championships in 1941 and 1942.

Palmberg showed his intellectual side in the three books he wrote and in his involvement in the Oregon community college system. His first book, titled *Copper Paladin: A Modoc Tragedy,* describes the resistance of the Modoc Indians when the U.S. Army tried to force them onto a reservation with the Klamath Indians. Next he published a collection of short stories called *Tavern Tales: The Lone Survivor and Other Stories.* In 1993 came a history of athletics in the Lower Columbia region titled *Toward One Flag,* in which he describes how sports can help to overcome ingrained hostilities among ethnic groups.

After coaching a few years in Astoria and in southern Oregon, Palmberg decided to pursue an advanced degree in education. He received a master's degree from Oregon State University and a doctorate from Washington State University, where his focus was community college development and administration. He used his education to help develop Blue Mountain Community College in Pendleton, Oregon, and he served as president of a community college in Wyoming.

Wally Palmberg (in white) coached his Astoria High School teams to state championships in 1941 and 1942. In 2010, his image still adorned the wall at Geno's Pizza and Burgers in Astoria.

By Alex Pajunis for the *Daily Astorian*.

Despite his intellectual accomplishments, Wally Palmberg is primarily remembered as one of the greatest basketball players and coaches in Astoria's history. Along with portraits of other athletes and teams of renown, his picture remains on prominent display at the sports-themed Geno's Pizza and Burgers on Leif Erikson Drive on the east side of town.

# Charles Haddix

By Liisa Penner

Charlie Haddix had a collection of feathers. When he wrote his friends, he often enclosed one along with directions to use it to tickle the spouse. His letters were always amusing, and it was a delight to find one in the mailbox. Remembering his youth in Astoria, he confessed that he had been the class clown.

The pranks Charlie played in school are legendary. One day when the teacher called roll, she came to Charlie's name and called it out. Charlie answered. The teacher looked around for him, but he wasn't in his seat. She called his name again, and again he answered. Finally she discovered Charlie hiding in an air shaft.

As a child, Charlie was curious about everything happening around him. He was present at every event. A photograph in the Heritage Museum collection shows a gathering of twins of all ages sitting on bleachers at a ball field in Astoria. A magnifying glass revealed that a lone boy at one end of the bleachers was Charlie Haddix.

In a photo of the Astoria city police dumping out confiscated liquor during Prohibition, Charlie was again on the scene.

Charlie had more friends than any-one I ever knew, in Astoria and all over

Young Charlie Haddix, ca. 1928.

CCHS 11711.507.

Astoria Twins Club, 1930. Charlie Haddix is in front of the post at left, the only child without a twin. CCHS 4456.14.

the world. Although he left Astoria when he joined the Merchant Marine in 1941, he continued to know everything that happened here. Once or twice a year, he came to Astoria for a visit, attending every Astoria High School reunion over a several-year period.

Charlie was a hard worker and clever. The history of the area especially intrigued him. He collected Astoria memorabilia, and he was happy to say that he had grown up poor but now had enough money to indulge his passion for collecting. He was proud that he had become successful through his own efforts.

Both Charlie's parents died in accidents in Astoria. When Charlie was still a child, a jack malfunctioned and his father was crushed beneath a house they were soon to move into. Charlie's mother, Mattie Haddix,

*When he wrote his friends, he often enclosed a feather along with directions to use it to tickle the spouse.*

had to make a living for herself and her two children. Friends found her work as a police matron. One of her duties was to monitor curfew violations, so she was gone in the evenings. Much of the time, Charlie was on his own. He contributed to the household income by delivering newspapers. Years later, Mattie was hit by a car and died of her injuries. Each visit to Astoria reminded Charlie of his losses.

Charles Haddix passed away in 1997, at the age of eighty-two. Once in a while, his feathers still float out of precious letters.

# Svenson Sisters

## By Nancy Hoffman

When Adaline Svenson, a retired secretary, died in 1993, Astorians were stunned to discover that she left an estate worth over a million dollars. Adaline was the last of three Svenson sisters.

Adaline, Medora, and Leila Svenson lived together frugally. They never married, never owned a car, and never purchased new appliances. Astorians

Leila and Adaline Svenson in front of their father's blacksmith shop in 1985. CCHS 26692.00S.

The Svenson family, ca. 1920. At left are Carl Svenson's wife, Ellen, and his youngest daughter, Medora; at right are Leila in back and Adaline in front. Robert Cummings Collection, CCHS.

recognized them because they dressed in colorful full-length coats and large hats as they walked, always together, from their home in Uppertown, the area east of Thirtieth Street, to their father's shop near the corner of Eighteenth and Exchange. Their passion was maintaining their father's blacksmith shop in meticulous condition.

Carl Svenson was born in Sweden but grew up in the state of Washington, where he learned the blacksmith trade. He came to Astoria in 1916 and five years later opened his shop. For the next forty-six years, he supported his family by hammering out metal over his fire and anvil. He designed and shaped wagon parts, horseshoes, automobile parts, and iron pieces needed by fishermen and farmers. He leased out the top of his building to automobile dealers and service shops, and he held meetings of the Socialist Labor Party amid his numerous books.

*Astorians were stunned to discover that Adaline left an estate worth over a million dollars.*

Carl continued to work into his eighties, but in 1967 he succumbed to a massive heart attack. His adoring daughters were devastated. Rather than clean

Carl Henning Svenson, ca. 1955. ROBERT CUMMINGS COLLECTION, CCHS.

out his shop, they closed the doors, leaving the tools exactly where he had last placed them, his coat hanging on its hook, the fire cold. Sixteen years later, in December 1985, Leila and Adaline were interviewed by the *Daily Astorian*. Leila said, "My dad could step in here and go to work." She added, "It was part of our lives for so many years, we just want to keep it."

*They closed the doors, leaving the tools exactly where he had last placed them, his coat hanging on its hook, the fire cold.*

For twenty-six years, the Svenson sisters regularly swept the shop and oiled Carl's machinery. Occasionally they permitted visitors to tour the preserved shop, but no one was allowed to disturb the tools or gear strewn about the room.

Medora died in 1984, and Leila and Adaline eventually decided to donate the shop and artifacts to the Clatsop County Historical Society along with $75,000 for its maintenance. A complete inventory of the contents was begun. But unfortunately, the two sisters never signed the necessary paperwork and died within four months of each other in 1993, Leila and then Adaline.

During probate after Adaline's death, the million-dollar estate was discovered along with an unsigned will. Distant relatives in America, Canada, and Sweden were contacted in the hope they would agree to the sisters' intentions as indicated in the will. The Swedish relatives declined, however, so the shop was put up for sale. Provisions of the sale required that Carl Svenson's blacksmith shop be preserved in the same condition for the next thirty years, until the year 2023. Randy Stemper, an Astoria businessman, agreed to those provisions and purchased the shop for $10,000.

Thanks to his daughters' persistence and love, Carl Svenson's shop exists to this day. It remains the way it was when the sisters died and is believed to be one of the few original early twentieth-century blacksmith shops to remain intact. It can be visited through private arrangements with the owner.

# Michael Foster

)(

## By M. J. Cody

Michael Foster was five years old when he acquired his first toy soldier. Besieged with bouts of pneumonia and allergies when he was young, he had to make weekly trips to Portland for allergy shots. He was promised that if he did not cry, he could choose something from the toy department at Meier & Frank.* He chose toy soldiers. Today, Foster still has those original lead soldiers, now a collectible army of a thousand.

Michael Foster (speaker at table on right) describing plans for the Clatsop County Historical Society's Heritage Museum to bankers and other businessmen, Astoria, ca. 1986. CCHS 1530.066.

---

*Meier & Frank department store was built in 1909. The tenth floor was a wonderland of toys. The May Company acquired the franchise in 1966. Its lower floors are currently home to Macy's department store, and upper floors have been converted to a boutique hotel, The Nines.

Michael Foster, 2010. By Alex Pajunas for the *Daily Astorian*.

The soldiers are not alone. Foster's four-story, 6,500-square-foot 1890s home is brimming with museum-quality collections. From inlaid snuffboxes and Victorian-era calling-card cases to Napoleon Bonaparte portraits and exquisite antique furniture juxtaposed with modern art, his beloved objects fill every square inch of space. His largest collection, Chinese porcelain, fills nearly three rooms.

*Foster bought his first piece of Chinese porcelain for a dollar fifty at a church rummage sale when he was eleven years old.*

Foster bought his first piece of Chinese porcelain for a dollar fifty at a church rummage sale when he was eleven years old. At the time, his parents looked at each other and said, "We don't stand a chance." When Foster brought home a second piece, they shook their heads and repeated the phrase.

"Why are you saying that?" asked Foster. They explained that his mother's father collected Chinese porcelain and his father's grandmother did likewise. Forces beyond his parents' control may have predisposed Foster's attraction to oriental colors and patterns.

Michael Foster, 2008. Courtesy of the Astoria Music Festival.

Foster is a fourth-generation Astorian. His grandfather, E. B. Foster, was Astoria's fire chief in the 1920s. During the 1922 fire, his grandfather felt obligated to save properties other than his own and lost everything.*

Born in 1940, Foster grew up in wartime Astoria, when U.S. Navy vessels frequented the port. His father supplied the ships with such staples as coffee, gelatin, and yeast, and Foster tagged along on deliveries.

"On my fourth birthday, the cake was a battleship," Foster recalled in a recent conversation. "Not a flat cake with a picture, but a huge structured cake with rolled black paper guns sticking out of it." He was allowed to attend USO entertainment—music revues, trained animal acts, and magic shows—at the U.S. Navy hospital and other venues in town. One Easter, a hundred and fifty sailors dyed Easter eggs for him, the only child they had contact with. "Imagine that giant bowl of colorful eggs!" Foster said, his face alight with the memory.

Gifted with a connoisseur's eye, Foster bought his first painting in high school. After graduating from Willamette University in Salem, Oregon, he wandered through Europe and the Middle East for nine months collecting treasures and shipping them home. He took a break from traveling, received his master's degree at the University of Oregon, and then, through USAID, taught at the American School in Kabul, Afghanistan, for four years, from 1966 to 1970.

"It was a wonderful time. Before the Russian invasion," recalled Foster. "I was invited to embassy parties and welcome to roam the king's gardens and orchards. I never locked my Volkswagen doors and would always find baskets of grapes and melons on my front seat when I returned from my rambles."

---

*When the city elected Ku Klux Klansman O. B. Setters mayor in 1923, E. B. Foster lost his job because he was Catholic—one of the groups, along with Jews, Chinese, and blacks, the Klan discriminated against. In 1927 a new mayor and city council were elected, and Foster was reinstated as fire chief.

Michael Foster at home, 2010. By Alex Pajunas for the *Daily Astorian*.

A suite on Foster's fourth floor displays some of the items from his years in Afghanistan—tribal carpets, paintings, colorful silks, silver and copper tea services, finely carved furniture, and ornate wood panels and pillars.

Foster returned to Astoria and taught history, then began a twenty-year stint as Astoria High School's librarian. After more than thirty years at the school, he retired.

In 2007 Foster was operated on for a benign brain tumor. Rehabilitation has been a long process, but he has recovered.

"I won't be traveling like I used to," said Foster. He will, however, continue to be active in Astoria, supporting the high school scholarship program he founded and continuing as a leader in the arts community. His downtown store, Michael's Antique & Art Gallery, is no more. But his new gallery, Astoria Fine Arts, opened in autumn 2009.

*"I was invited to embassy parties and welcome to roam the king's gardens and orchards."*

Foster's fondness for splendid objects is obvious as he pats cherry-wood or walnut Victorian furniture pieces when he passes them, or his eyes twinkle in delight as he points out his cherished Rose Medallion Chinese porcelain. Asked in 2009 how many pieces of art he owns, he said, "3,600 have been catalogued." There are more, but he doesn't know how many.

About his obsession with collecting, Foster said, "It's like a disease. It's similar to alcoholism, except you feel better."

# Liisa Penner

## By M. J. Cody

Liisa Penner has an uncanny ability to recall Astoria's past as though she has lived it. As archivist for the Clatsop County Historical Society's Heritage Museum, Penner can remember and connect families and facts, readily evoking historic associations and incidents. Penner says her gift of recall has a drawback:

Liisa Penner working with the collections of the Clatsop County Historical Society, 2010. By Alex Pajunas for the *Daily Astorian*.

she focuses on and absorbs details so strongly that she often loses sight of other things. "Don't ask me about anything current," Penner says. "I have a terrible memory." But when she writes things down, such as historic events or even small details transcribed from early journals or newspaper accounts, they register as deeply as personal experience.

"People and things that happened in history are real to me," she says.

Penner was born in Finland in 1940 to a Finnish mother, Helmi, and American father, Charles Mellin. A year later, Helmi and Liisa joined Mellin in the U.S. Penner's sister, Karen Mellin, was born in Chicago. The family spent the World War II years in Hermosa Beach, California, where her father worked in nearby shipyards. After the war, Mellin left the family to seek employment wherever he could find it, traveling to Alaska, Hawaii, and throughout the continental United States. He never returned to Helmi, leaving her to fend for herself and the girls. Helmi took a job with a wealthy family as a live-in cook and temporarily placed Liisa and Karen with friends. Over the next six years, the girls barely saw their mother and were shuttled among family friends and their father's relatives.

*"Don't ask me about anything current," Penner says. "I have a terrible memory."*

In 1951, Helmi and her best friend, Hilda, decided to visit Hilda's sister in Brownsmead, Oregon, near Astoria. Helmi retrieved her daughters, and they made the trip north by bus. On that vacation, Helmi fell in love with a small restaurant in Astoria, and the two friends decided to set up their own café. Helmi left the girls with Hilda's sister and family, which Penner recalls as one of the best times of her young life.

Helmi returned with a car full of her worldly goods, gathered the girls, moved to Astoria, and set up the Koffee Kup café. Helmi and Hilda's partnership foundered, but Helmi, as sole owner, kept the business going for twenty-seven years. During their school years, Liisa and Karen were reunited with their father and spent summer vacations with him and their stepmother in Red Lodge, Montana.

Penner spent one year at the University of Oregon in Eugene, Oregon, before marrying coast guardsman Henry Penner, who was stationed in Astoria.

They soon had two children, a boy and a girl. Penner returned to her studies for a year at Clatsop College, then the family moved to Eugene so she could work toward a master's degree in anthropology.

"I thought I wanted to be an archaeologist, working on sites in the Middle East or Europe," Penner recalls. On a three-month trip in 1970, Penner, her husband, and the kids visited family in Finland and drove south to Rome, where the whole family was sick. "That was enough for me," Penner says. "We headed straight north to Switzerland, where we found we much preferred the thunderstorms to the heat in Rome. There was no way I could stand being an archaeologist in hot climates."

Archivist Liisa Penner at the Clatsop County Historical Society's Heritage Museum, 2010. By Alex Pajunas for the *Daily Astorian*.

Liisa (Arlene E.) Penner, ca. 2007. PHOTO BY KATE RAMBEAU.

Penner finished her master's degree in Eugene, and the family resettled in Astoria. Henry worked in a welding machine shop and Penner at varying jobs in social services. When their third child, the youngest daughter, reached school age in 1983, a class at Clatsop College on preserving art and historic materials helped catapult Penner into what would become her life's work. She began working with collections for the Clatsop County Historical Society, transcribing historic documents and archiving, and she spent a couple of winters doing inventory at the Flavel House.

*❧ "It was terribly cold, but I was afraid to turn on the heat. I didn't want to be responsible for burning the house down." ☙*

"It was terribly cold, but I was afraid to turn on the heat," says Penner. "I didn't want to be responsible for burning the house down."

She became active in the Clatsop County Genealogy Society, resulting in several index books of local research materials. At first she was nervous about responding to queries for the museum of the Clatsop County Historical Society. "I was so afraid of answering queries," says Penner. "I didn't think I was prepared."

Penner realized there was a dire need for historical source material and began to copy census information, putting together a "who's who" index of early pioneers. She especially remembers the joy of helping transcribe a journal written by Preston W. Gillette, an unusually detailed account of the 1850s.

"By putting everything on cards, writing information over and over, I get to know each person as an individual," says Penner.

Penner has been the editor of the historical society's quarterly *Cumtux* since 1992, publishing over sixty issues. Stories from historic newspaper accounts that caught her interest resulted in the collection *Salmon Fever: River's End: Tragedies on the Lower Columbia River in the 1870s, 1880s, and 1890s,* published in 2006. Penner and her husband were married for fifty years and are now separated. Her grown children all live and work in the Northwest. She is the grandmother of three and the great-grandmother of three.

"I don't know quite how to do the right thing socially, and I find it difficult to talk to people," says Penner. "History is the one subject I can talk about. It's an obsession, and hard to talk about anything else."

Penner's enthusiasm for her subject and her deep insight make the Clatsop County Historical Society and its Heritage Museum a haven for researchers. Some archivists see themselves as gatekeepers, projecting an attitude of exclusion. Penner is generous with her time and knowledge. This book would not have come together without Liisa Penner's devotion to the stories of Astoria and the collections of the Clatsop County Historical Society.

# Robert Adams

## By M. J. Cody

Photographer Robert Adams was born in New Jersey in 1937, moved to Colorado as a teenager, attended college in California, and returned to Colorado to teach. Since 1997, Adams and his wife, Kerstin, have lived in Astoria. Adams' westward journey has informed his life and his life's work.

Adams has documented scenes of the American West for forty years, revealing the impact of human presence on natural landscapes. Working in black and white, he became prominent as part of the photographic movement known as New Topographics. He has produced many books and won several prestigious photography awards, including two Guggenheim Memorial Foundation Fellowships (1973 and 1980), a MacArthur Foundation Fellowship (1994), and most recently, the 2009 Hasselblad Award. Major exhibitions have included the San Francisco Museum of Modern Art and the Museum of Modern Art in New York.

The Adamses live in a home high above the city overlooking the Columbia River. At age seventy-three, Robert Adams is soft-spoken and thoughtful, yet ardent in his views. He was in his twenties when his love for photography and his passion for environmental stewardship became an entwined focus.

"When I returned to Colorado from college in the late 1950s, I was devastated," Adams said in a January 2009 interview, recalling his awakening to a painful reality. "I climbed mountains. I hunted. I fished. I loved the outdoors. But when I came back, there was a huge development boom, and many things I loved were destroyed. I wanted to be part of saving it."

About that time, a friend came back from the Korean War with a 35 mm camera and showed Adams how to use it. "He said photography was great fun, and indeed it was. But it became something else, too. Colleagues thought I was losing it. I had a secure teaching job at the University of Southern Colorado—a nice office, steady hours, summers off. How could I leave it to take photographs?"

Robert Adams at home in Astoria, 2010. By Alex Pajunas for the *Daily Astorian*.

Astoria, Oregon, with the Columbia River and Tongue Point at right, 2004.

Adams admired the work of Lewis Hine, the early twentieth-century photographer who helped to expose grim working conditions in American factories and mines. "Hine said that photography can show two things: what is right, so we can value it; and what is wrong, so we can change it. I like to document what's glorious in the West and remains glorious, despite what we've done to it. But I also want to show what is disturbing and needs correction. A very big part of why we're here in Astoria is our concern for this beautiful place."

Adams and his wife first visited Astoria in the 1960s. "Right from the beginning, we felt there was something special here," Adams said. "It has to do with the mystery of this great river meeting the sea. We felt the spirit of the place and

PHOTO BY ROBERT ADAMS, TAKEN FROM HIS FRONT PORCH. COURTESY OF ROBERT ADAMS.

deeply wanted to live here, but we couldn't figure out how we could swing it. We finally made the move thirty years later, thanks to Kerstin's retirement and a MacArthur fellowship."

He spent time photographing con-ventionally beautiful coastal scenes. As the bicentennial year of the Lewis and Clark Expedition approached, Adams felt his real job was to remind people of the devastation taking place. "The country had great hopes for the American West," he said. "But we're squandering our great resources—our fisheries, our

*"Right from the beginning, we felt there was something special here."*

Robert Adams at home in Astoria, 2010. By Alex Pajunas for the *Daily Astorian*.

forests. There is an exhaustion of spirit. I can see it amidst my fellow citizens in this small town and in this region. Many go to great lengths not to see or to confront what is happening."

An influx of newcomers has energized Astoria in recent years. Once a bustling maritime province with cannery piers defining the waterfront, the town languished for years as fish populations diminished and fishing was no longer a prime industry. But Astoria's location and its authentic character appealed to those seeking a life less hectic and more connected to the natural environment. Like many who have migrated to the area, the Adamses feel a profound commitment to their new home.

*"We love this place. But with the gift comes great responsibility."*

"We love this place," Adams said. "Walking in the woods, on the beach, in town, you sense what a gift you've been given. But with the gift comes great responsibility. Astoria is at the confluence of very serious environmental issues. We've got to try to fix it, but not lose heart. With the photos and the books, I believed I could say something important about this grand and special place and help to save it. I still believe that."

# About the Authors

M. J. CODY is co-editor with Mike Houck of the acclaimed *Wild in the City: A Guide to Portland Metropolitan Greenspaces,* author of *Our Portland,* a coffee table–style book with photographer Rick Schafer, and editor of *Best Places to Stay: Pacific Northwest* (6th edition). An Oregon native, Cody spent many years in L.A., where she was the photo editor of the *L.A. Weekly* and an award-winning magazine art director for the TeleFlora Corporation. She worked on television shows including "Major Dad," "Mama's Family," and "Knots Landing," for which she won the Soap Opera Award for "Best Storyline" two consecutive years. Cody has a regular column, "Sleeping Around the Northwest," which appears in the *Oregonian*'s Sunday travel section. She has contributed features to the *Oregonian,* the *Seattle Times, Horizon Air, NW Palate Magazine, Audubon Magazine, Travel Oregon,* and other publications. She has researched, written, and produced two audio driving-tour CDs, "The Barlow Road" and "A Feast for the Senses," and written TeleTales, a series of stories for Oregon's Mt. Hood Territory, accessible by cell phone at Clackamas County heritage sites. Currently she is working on the second edition of *Wild in the City.*

AMY HOFFMAN COUTURE grew up in northern California. She moved to Astoria as a teenager and graduated from Astoria High School. She earned a bachelor's degree in history from the University of Oregon and a master's degree in history from Minnesota State University in Mankato, where she focused on nineteenth-century social and labor history in the United States and Britain. Her thesis was a comparison of ancient mining laws in Cornwall, England, with the mining codes established in California's gold camps in the 1860s. Couture also holds a master's degree in teacher education and taught fifth grade for three years in Stebbins, Alaska, before taking several years off to stay home with her two young sons. Currently she lives in Ashland, Oregon, with her husband and children.

JOHN E. GOODENBERGER grew up in Astoria, Oregon, and returned to his hometown after receiving a Bachelor of Architecture from the University of Oregon. He served thirteen years as a historic building consultant for the City of Astoria, recording the history of more than six hundred local buildings while educating the public about the stylistic and historical importance of their houses and commercial structures. In addition to being a preservation consultant for Jay Raskin Architects, Goodenberger writes a column for the *Daily Astorian* called "Great City Rising," a monthly discussion of architecture and history. He is a regional advisor for the Historic Preservation League of Oregon and a founding member and current president of the Lower Columbia Preservation Society. John has served as caretaker and docent for the Captain George Flavel House Museum, participated in the museum's restoration, and performed living history as Captain Flavel.

NANCY RICKER HOFFMAN grew up in Sacramento, a fourth-generation Californian. She attended UC Davis and worked in several state agencies before returning to school and earning a master's degree in English. She then moved with her family to Astoria in order to work for Clatsop Community College as an English instructor. She taught composition, literature, and humanities and participated in a local writing group and local book group. Her poetry has appeared in a few literary magazines, and she also joined with three other women in publishing a book of poetry about mothers and daughters. After retiring from the college, she began a new adventure by attending Lewis and Clark Law School in Portland. She graduated in May 2010 and plans to set up a law practice in Astoria.

LIISA PENNER was born in Finland. She moved to the U.S. as a child, eventually coming to Astoria in 1951. After graduating from Astoria High School, she attended the University of Oregon, where she received her master's degree in Anthropology. Upon returning to the Astoria area, she became active in the Clatsop County Genealogy Society, working with its members to produce several books of local research materials. About the same time, she began working with the collections at the Clatsop County Historical Society and was given the task of monitoring accessions and responding to queries. Discovering a serious need for making historical source material available for researchers, she began collecting, abstracting, and printing this material. She has worked as editor of the historical society's quarterly *Cumtux* since 1992. Penner is now Archivist for the Clatsop County Historical Society at the Heritage Museum.

CALVIN TRILLIN was born and raised in Kansas City, Missouri. He graduated from Yale in 1957, did a hitch in the army, then joined *Time* magazine. In 1963, he became a staff writer for the *New Yorker*. From 1978 through 1985, he was also a columnist for the *Nation*. Two collections of his columns were published: *Uncivil Liberties* (1982) and *With All Disrespect* (1985). Trillin has published three books on eating (the "tummy trilogy"): *American Fried, Third Helpings,* and *Alice, Let's Eat*. He has appeared on television in such shows as "Today," "The Tonight Show," and "Late Night with David Letterman." In 1998 he published *Family Man,* a memoir of his experiences as husband and father. He has also written comic verse, three comic novels, and a collection of short stories. His latest publication is *Deciding the Next Decider: The 2008 Presidential Race in Rhyme* (comic verse with commentary, 2008).

# Index

Adair, John, 71, 76
Adams, Kerstin, 210, 211, 212, 213
Adams, Robert, 210–214
Alderbrook, 59
AMCCO (Astoria Marine Construction Company), 156, 168, 169, 171, 172
Andrew Young house, 151
Astor, John Jacob, 8, 11, 53, 73
Astoria Column, 41, 127, 146n
Astoria Finnish Evangelical Lutheran Church, 134
Astoria High School, 154, 172, 197, 205
  Wally Palmberg at, 193, 194, 195
Astoria Law Enforcement League, 137
Astoria Marine Construction Company (AMCCO), 156, 168, 169, 171, 172
Astoria-Megler Bridge, 157
Astoria Regatta, 110, 112, 135, 172
Astoria Twins Club, 197

Baker, George L., 163
bar pilots. *See* Columbia bar pilots
Barbey, Graham, 8
Barnes, Jane, 9, 54, 55–58
Barry, Margaret Grant, 99
Basch, Richard, 46, 51
Bay, Anna, 147–150
Bay, Jacob O. "Jack," 148, 149, 150
Bay, Matthew, 149

Bell, Anna Louise "Pinky" Reid Carlson, 177, 178
Bell, Burnby Scott McKean, 141, 142, 176–179
Bell, Harry, 142, 177
Bell, Polly McKean, 94, 141–143, 177
Bell, Thomas McKean, 178
Bernier, Constance, 142
Bernier, Harry, 177
Bing, Rudolf, 35
Birnie, James, 67, 68
Blue Mountain Community College, 195
Brallier, Henry, 109
Bridger, Jim, 78
Brown, Ebba Wicks, 151, 152
Brown, Hiram, 89
Buchanan, John A., 128–130
Buchanan, Louise, 128
Buchanan, Madge Ragsdale, 128
Buchanan, Maurine, 128
Bumble Bee Seafoods, 111

California Gold Rush, 76, 89, 91
Carlson, Anna Louise "Pinky" Reid, 177, 178
Carlson, Edwin, 178
Cassakas (son of Chinook chief Comcomly), 58
Cederberg, Maria, 151
Champ, John W., 88
Champoeg public meeting (1843), 79
Chessman, Merle, 161
Chinese in Astoria, 11
Chinook Indians, 45, 49, 54, 66, 179. *See also* Cassakas; Comcomly
Chinook Jargon, 74

Christensen, B. J., 190
Churchill, Dorothy, 191, 192
Churchill, Sam, 190–193
Civil War, 12, 24, 89, 96, 102–103. *See also names of military leaders*
Clark, William, 45, 46, 48, 49, 51, 85. *See also* Corps of Discovery; Fort Clatsop; Lewis and Clark salt cairn
*Clatsop Chief* (sternwheeler), 131
Clatsop Community College, 154, 208, 209
Clatsop County Historical Society, 18, 54, 76, 141, 152, 193, 209
  Flavel House Museum and, 167
  Fort Clatsop replica and, 176
  Heritage Museum of, 174, 196, 202, 206, 208, 210
  Nivala scrapbooks held by, 181
  Svenson blacksmith shop and, 201
Clatsop Indians, 45–52, 54, 84–87 passim, 107. *See also* Coboway; Shortess, Ann; Smith, Celiast; Smith, Charlotte; Smith, Silas; Smith, Solomon
Clatsop Plains Pioneer Presbyterian Church, 75, 77, 79
Coboway, Clatsop chief, 45–52, 73, 108
Columbia bar pilots, 12, 67, 92, 93, 189. *See also individual names*

Columbia Defense League, 165

Columbia River Maritime Museum, 41, 172, 174, 176, 190, 193
Shark Rock at, 129

Columbia River One Design (CROD) yacht, 170, 172

Columbia River Packers Association, 111

Columbia River Yachting Association, 171

Comcomly, Chinook chief, 58, 66, 178, 179

Connall, Des, 28, 30, 38

Corps of Discovery, 45–50 passim. *See also* Clark, William; Fort Clatsop; Lewis, Meriwether

crimping (shanghaiing), 99, 100, 101, 118

CROD (Columbia River One Design) yacht, 170, 172

Crosby, Alfred, 92

Crosby, Bing, 124

Crosby, Lillian, 124

Curtis, C. J., 159

Dart, Anson, 86, 87

Dernbach, Father Arthur, 27

Dershowitz, Alan, 36, 37

Dever, Lem, 160–163

DeVos, Peter, 67

Diamond, Charles T., 153

Dix, Mary Augusta, 78, 80, 81

Dodge, Charles, 109

Donation Land Act (1850), 64, 86

Drake, Lee D., 161

Driskoll, Tim, 168

Drouillard, George, 49

Dunbar, Frank I., 123–126

Dyer, Genevieve "Geno" Thompson, 169, 170, 171

Dyer, Joe, 168–172

Dyer, Tom, 172

Edwards, Charles, 92

Effler, George, 109

Elfving, Fritz, 154–157, 169

*Eliza Anderson* (paddlewheeler), 93

Elliott, Olivia, 72

Elliott, Susan, 70, 71, 72

Erickson, August, 8, 118–121

Erickson, F. C., 150

Erickson, Gustafa, 120

Erickson, Hilda M., 150

Erickson, Maria, 121

Erickson's Saloon, 118, 120

Faber, Glenn, 28, 30, 38

Farnsworth, Asa Cole, 92

Ferguson, David James, 164–165

Finkelstein, Rachel, 146

Finkelstein, Toba, 146

Finnish Socialist Club, 138

First Presbyterian Church, 23, 129, 164

Fisher, Ezra, 71

Flathead Indians, 47, 78. *See also* Chinook Indians; Clatsop Indians; head flattening

Flavel, Florence Sherman (wife of Harry M.), 18, 21–43 passim

Flavel, George Conrad (son of the Captain), 13, 14, 15, 18, 24

Flavel, George S. (the Captain), 12, 13, 23, 24, 38, 93, 105

Flavel, Harry Melville (grandson of the Captain), 18, 21, 24

Flavel, Harry Sherman (great-grandson of the Captain; son of Harry M. and Florence), 7, 21–43 passim

Flavel, Katie (daughter of the Captain), 13, 15, 16, 22, 36

Flavel, Mary Christina (wife of the Captain), 12, 13, 16, 17

Flavel, Mary Louise (daughter of Harry M. and Florence), 18, 21–43 passim

Flavel, Nellie (daughter of the Captain), 13, 14, 15, 16, 22, 36
Marshall J. Kinney and, 109, 112

Flavel, Patricia, 15

Flavel family, 11–43. *See also individual names*

Flavel House Museum, 15, 16, 17, 23, 41, 141, 209
May Miller and, 167
skull of Comcomly displayed at, 179

Fort Astoria, 52, 85, 129, 141

Fort Clatsop, 46, 48, 49, 85, 96, 141
replicas of, 175, 176, 177, 179

Fort George, 51, 53, 54, 67, 73
American settlers' conflict with, 65, 68, 69
Jane Barnes at, 55, 57, 58

Fort Stevens, 46, 128

Fort Stevens State Park, 73

Fort Vancouver, 64, 67, 70, 73, 74, 84

Foster, E. B. "Ed," 162, 204

Foster, Michael, 202–206

Foster, Sam, 167

Fuchs, Netta, 144

Fuchs, Velvel, 144, 145

Fulton, Charles William, 115–118
Fulton, Clyde, 115
Fulton, Fred, 21

Gairdner, Meredith, 178
Gass, Patrick, 47
Gearhart, Oregon, 112, 115
Gearhart, Philip, 112
George C. Flavel house, 18, 23, 41
Gerttula, Steven, 28, 37, 38, 39, 40
Gervais, Joseph, 74
Gifford, Fred, 160, 162
Gillette, Preston W., 95–97, 209
Goodenberger, John, 42
Gold Rush, 76, 89, 91
Gottlieb, Charles, 150
*Governor Newell* (sternwheeler), 131
Grace Episcopal Church, 72, 90, 142
Grant, Alex, 99
Grant, Bridget, 9, 98–101
Grant, Ignatius (Nace), 99, 158, 159
Grant, John F. (Jack), 99, 100
Grant, Kate, 99, 101
Grant, Margaret, 99, 101
Grant, Mary Ellen, 99, 101
Grant, Peter, Sr., 98
Grant, Peter, Jr., 99, 100
Grant, Ulysses S., 89
Grant, William, 99
Gray, Caroline, 81
Gray, Mary Augusta Dix, 78, 81
Gray, William H., 76, 77–81, 125
Great Depression, 166, 171, 179
great fire in Astoria (1922), 129, 138, 149, 153, 162

E. B. Foster and, 204
Joe Dyer and, 169

Haddix, Charles, 196–198
Haddix, Mattie, 197, 198
Halloran, John T., 94, 106
Hansel, Barbara, 9
Harley, Francis Clay, 9, 158–159
Harvey, Edward, 187–188
head flattening (Chinook and Clatsop Indian custom), 47, 48
Hebrew Immigrant Aid Society (HIAS), 145
Henry, Alexander, 51, 54, 57
Heritage Museum, 174, 196, 202, 206, 208, 210
HIAS (Hebrew Immigrant Aid Society), 145
Hill, Charles, 130, 131
Hill, Minnie, 130–132
Hine, Lewis, 212
Hines, Jerome, 23, 34, 35
Hines, Lucia Evangelista, 34
Hoag, R. Doane, 32
Hobson, John, 125
Hooker, Joseph, 89
Hope, James L., 137, 138
Hudson's Bay Company, 52, 57, 65, 67, 68, 88
  attack on Clatsop village by, 84–85
  John Shively and, 70
  relocation from Fort George to Fort Vancouver, 73
  Solomon Smith and, 108
Hummasti, Paul George, 138
Hustler, Eliza McKean, 93, 94
Hustler, J. G., 63, 91–94, 125

Ingalls, Sylvester, 109
Ingleton, Jim, 134, 135

Ingleton, Rose, 134–136
Irving, Washington, 11
*Isaac Todd* (British sailing ship), 53, 54, 55, 57

J. D. H. Gray house, 187, 188
*Jane A. Falkenberg* (barkentine), 93, 94
Jeffers, Elijah, 97
Jeffers, Joseph, 96, 97
Johnson, LaRee, 42
Johnson, Martha Ann, 70
Josephson, Alec, 26, 27, 29, 30, 37, 39
Juhrs, Kate (descendant of Clatsop chief Coboway), 51

Kamm, Caroline Gray, 81
Kamm, Jacob, 81
Karchoff, Theodore, 150
Keith, James, 58
Kelly, "Bunco," 148
Kelly, William, 158, 159
Kinney, Alfred C., 111, 112–113
Kinney, Eliza, 110
Kinney, Lyman, 111
Kinney, Margaretta Morgan, 110, 112
Kinney, Marshall J., 109–112, 115
Kinney, Narcissa White, 112, 114–115
Kinney, Robert, 110
Kinney, William, 111
Kinney Cannery, 110, 111
KKK (Ku Klux Klan), 136, 137, 138, 160–163 passim, 204n
Klamath Indians, 195
Klep, Alice Latture, 173, 176
Klep, Rolf, 8, 172–176
Koffee Kup café, 186, 207
Kratz, O. A., 162

Ku Klux Klan (KKK), 136, 137, 138, 160–163 passim, 204n

Labo, Flavanio, 35
Lane, Joseph, 76
Lantto, Hilma, 134
Lattie, Alexander, 65, 66–69
Lattie, Marie Catherine Sikkas, 67, 68, 69
Latture, Alice, 173, 176
Lemon, Mary Ellen Grant, 99
Lewis, Meriwether, 45, 48, 49, 50, 51, 213. *See also* Corps of Discovery; Fort Clatsop; Lewis and Clark salt cairn
Lewis and Clark salt cairn, 85, 87
Lighter, Kate Grant, 99
Linenweber, Christian, 77
Livingston, Neil, 135, 136
Louvre Saloon, 8, 119, 120
*Lurline* (steamship), 189

Mansker, Acme "Ac," 168, 169
Mansker, Clair, 168, 169
Martin, Charles H., 165
Martineau, Michel, 86
*Mary Taylor* (pilot boat), 93
McAlpin, Kenneth, 8
McCall, Tom, 7, 8
McClure, John, 63–66, 68, 69, 74, 82
McClure, John (Jean) Archibald Concomlly, 66
McClure, Louisa, 64, 66
McDonald, John, 54, 55, 56
McKean, A. B., 90
McKean, Eliza, 93, 94
McKean, Mary Jane Smith, 141, 142
McKean, Samuel T., Jr., 142

McKean, Samuel T., Sr., 141
McLoughlin, John, 70, 74, 84, 85, 86
McMillan, Anna. *See* Anna Bay
McTavish, Donald, 52–54, 55, 56
McTavish, John George, 53
McTavish, Simon, 52
Mellin, Charles, 185, 186, 207
Mellin, Helmi Huttunen, 183–186, 207
Mellin, Karen, 185, 186, 207
Mellin, Liisa (Arlene E.). *See* Penner, Liisa (Arlene E.)
Mercer, Asa, 141
*Merrimac* (cabin cruiser), 168, 171
Michel, Jennie (Tsin-is-tum), 84–87
Miller, May Spexarth, 166–168
*Minnie Hill* (sternwheeler), 131
Modoc Indians, 195
*Monterey* (steamship), 189
Morgan, Margaretta, 110, 112
Morrison, R. W., 76
Mossman, Minnie Mae, 130–132
Murtagh, Henry, 129

Naab, Michael, 174
Nivala, Emil Richard "Dic," 179–183
Norris Staples house, 152
*North Beach* (ferry), 156, 157
North West Fur Company, 51, 52, 53, 54, 55

Olney, Cyrus, 66, 72, 81–83
Olney, Nathan, 81, 82
Olney, Sarah, 82

Ordway, John, 50
Oregon Historical Society, 85, 141, 178, 190
"Oregon, My Oregon," 128
Oregon Pioneer and Historical Society, 76, 125
Oregon Society of Artists, 137
Oregon State Board of Health, 113
Oregon State Medical Society, 113
Oregon State University, 169, 193, 195
Oregon State University Seafood lab, 187
Oregon Trail, 70, 88
*Oregonian,* 37, 121, 144, 145
Orloff, Chet, 8
Orne, Martin T., 36
Otto Owen house, 153

Pacific Fur Company, 11, 53, 73, 85
Palmberg, Walter "Wally," 193–195
Parker, W. W., 148
Parnassus Books, 9
*Peacock* (shipwreck), 74
Pendleton, Oregon, 7, 8, 195
Pendleton Round-Up, 8
Penner, Henry, 207
Penner, Liisa (Arlene E.), 185, 186, 206–210
Pierce, Franklin, 82
Pierce, Walter M., 163
Point Adams, 73, 86
Poirier, Basile, 73
Powers, Mary, 75, 77
Powers, Truman, 75–77, 79, 125
Prohibition, 121, 196

Quinn, B. J. Christensen, 190

Quinn, Edgar, 189–190

*Raccoon* (British naval
frigate), 53, 54, 55, 56
Ragsdale, Madge, 128
Raunio, Kalle (Flint), 139
Raunio, Maria, 138–141
Renninger, Kandy, 25
Riippa, Andrew, 132
Riippa, Charles, 132
Riippa, Hilma Lantto, 133
Riippa, Jacob, 132, 133, 134
Riippa, Joseph, 132–134
Rissanen, Aku, 141
Rockwell, Cleveland, 94,
102–106
Rockwell, Cornelia (Neely),
104, 106
Rockwell, Cornelia
Flemming Russell, 104,
106
Rockwell, Gertrude Ellinor,
104, 106
Rogers, Moses, 92
Ross Opera House, 8
Russell, Cornelia Flemming,
104, 106

Saarinen, Erlund, 139
Saarinen, Maria. *See* Maria
Raunio
Salin, Eetu, 139
*San Francisco Chronicle,*
150
Santa Fe Trail, 64
Sardos, James, 35
Savoy Saloon, 147
Schacht, Emil, 119, 124
Schnitzer, Arlene Director,
146n
Schnitzer, Avrum, 144
Schnitzer, Jordan, 146n
Schnitzer, Rachel (Rosa,
Rose) Finkelstein, 146
Schnitzer, Sam, 143–146
Schnitzer, Tauba, 144

Seaside, Oregon, 85, 87,
112, 122, 127
Setters, O. B., 161, 204
Seward, William, 80
Shane, Carlos W., 96
shanghaiing (crimping), 99,
100, 101, 118
*Shark* (shipwreck), 74, 76,
88, 129
Shark Rock, 129
Sheridan, Philip, 89
Sherman, Florence, 18,
21–43 passim
Sherman, William
Tecumseh, 103, 104
Shively, Charles, 70, 72
Shively, Cyrus, 71
Shively, John, 63, 69–72
Shively, Joseph, 71
Shively, Martha Ann
Johnson, 70
Shively, Susan Elliott, 70,
71, 72
Shortess, Ann, 59
Shortess, Robert, 59–62
Sikkas, Marie Catherine, 67,
68, 69
Sioux Indians, 78
Smith, Celiast (Helen), 52,
72–75, 108
Smith, Charlotte, 75,
107–109
Smith, Helen (Celiast), 52,
72–75, 108
Smith, Mary Jane, 141, 142
Smith, Silas B., 51, 52, 74,
96, 108, 125
Smith, Solomon, 52, 72–75,
79, 108
Social Democratic Party,
139, 140, 141
Socialist Labor Party, 199
Spalding, Henry, 78
Spexarth, August, 166
Spexarth, Mary Alice, 166
Spexarth, May, 166–168

Stanford University, 142,
151, 177
Stemper, Randy, 201
Sullivan, John, 100
Sutter, John, 78
Sutter's Fort, 78
Svenson, Adaline, 198–201
passim
Svenson, Carl Henning,
199, 200
Svenson, Ellen, 199
Svenson, Leila, 198–201
passim
Svenson, Medora, 198–201
passim
Svenson blacksmith shop,
199, 201
Svenson sisters (Adaline,
Medora, and Leila),
198–201

Thompson, Genevieve
"Geno," 169, 170, 171
Tostum, Chief (nephew of
Coboway), 50, 51
*Tourist 1* (ferry), 155, 172
*Tourist 2* (ferry), 156, 157
*Tourist 3* (ferry), 156, 157,
169
*Toveri* (Comrade), 140, 141
*Toveritar* (Woman
Comrade), 140
Trask, Eldridge, 68
Trillin, Calvin, 7, 9
Tsin-is-tum (Jennie
Michel), 84–87

University of Oregon, 137,
172, 191, 204, 207
Uniontown, 20, 23, 27, 123
Uppertown, 20, 199

Van Dusen, Adam, 88–91, 125
Van Dusen, Caroline, 88,
90, 91
Van Dusen, Willis, 91

Van Dusen family, 90

Wadhams, William, 77
Wah-tat-kum, Nehalem
  chief, 86
Waiilatpu (Whitman
  Mission), 77, 78, 80,
  81, 93
War of 1812, 53
Warrenton, Oregon, 66, 79,
  84, 143
Washington State
  University, 195
WCTU (Women's Christian
  Temperance Union),
  114, 115, 162
Weister, George M., 85
*Western American,* 160, 161,
  162

White, Cornelius, 93
White, Narcissa, 112
Whitman, Marcus, 78, 80
Whitman, Narcissa, 78, 80
Whitman Mission
  (Waiilatpu), 77, 78, 80,
  81, 93
Wicks, Ebba, 151, 152
Wicks, Esther, 151, 152
Wicks, Ethel, 151
Wicks, John E., 151–154
Wicks, Maria Cederberg,
  151
Willamette University, 136,
  204
Willard, Charles, 117, 118,
  122, 123
*William and Anne*
  (shipwreck), 84–85

Williams, Jack, 121–123. *See
  also* Willard, Charles
Wilson, Albert E., 63
Wire, Melville T., 136–138
Wise, Herman, 126–127
Women's Christian
  Temperance Union
  (WCTU), 114, 115, 162
women's suffrage, 138
World War I, 128, 164, 169
World War II, 20, 183, 189,
  191, 204, 207
  Burnby Bell's service in,
    177
  minesweepers built by
    AMCCO, 168, 171
  Rolf Klep's service in, 175
Wyeth, Nathaniel, 73